Mastering Git

Mastering Computer Science
Series Editor: Sufyan bin Uzayr

Mastering Git: A Beginner's Guide
Sumanna Kaul, Shahryar Raz, and Divya Sachdeva

Mastering Ruby on Rails: A Beginner's Guide
Mathew Rooney and Madina Karybzhanova

Mastering Sketch: A Beginner's Guide
Mathew Rooney and Md Javed Khan

Mastering C#: A Beginner's Guide
Mohamed Musthafa MC, Divya Sachdeva, and Reza Nafim

Mastering GitHub Pages: A Beginner's Guide
Sumanna Kaul and Shahryar Raz

Mastering Unity: A Beginner's Guide
Divya Sachdeva and Aruqqa Khateib

For more information about this series, please visit: https://www.routledge.com/Mastering-Computer-Science/book-series/MCS

The "Mastering Computer Science" series of books are authored by the Zeba Academy team members, led by Sufyan bin Uzayr.

Zeba Academy is an EdTech venture that develops courses and content for learners primarily in STEM fields, and offers education consulting to Universities and Institutions worldwide. For more info, please visit https://zeba.academy

Mastering Git

A Beginner's Guide

Edited by Sufyan bin Uzayr

CRC Press
Taylor & Francis Group
Boca Raton   London   New York

CRC Press is an imprint of the
Taylor & Francis Group, an **informa** business

First edition published 2022
by CRC Press
6000 Broken Sound Parkway NW, Suite 300, Boca Raton, FL 33487-2742

and by CRC Press
2 Park Square, Milton Park, Abingdon, Oxon, OX14 4RN

CRC Press is an imprint of Taylor & Francis Group, LLC

© 2022 Sufyan bin Uzayr

ISBN: 9781032134161 (hbk)
ISBN: 9781032134154 (pbk)
ISBN: 9781003229100 (ebk)

DOI: 10.1201/9781003229100

Typeset in Minion
by KnowledgeWorks Global Ltd.

Contents

About the Editor

Sufyan bin Uzayr is a writer, coder, and entrepreneur with more than a decade of experience in the industry. He has authored several books in the past, pertaining to a diverse range of topics, ranging from History to Computers/IT.

Sufyan is the Director of Parakozm, a multinational IT company specializing in EdTech solutions. He also runs Zeba Academy, an online learning and teaching vertical with a focus on STEM fields.

Sufyan specializes in a wide variety of technologies, such as JavaScript, Dart, WordPress, Drupal, Linux, and Python. He holds multiple degrees, including ones in Management, IT, Literature, and Political Science.

Sufyan is a digital nomad, dividing his time between four countries. He has lived and taught in universities and educational institutions around the globe. Sufyan takes a keen interest in technology, politics, literature, history, and sports, and in his spare time, he enjoys teaching coding and English to young students.

Learn more at sufyanism.com.

Getting Started

IN THIS CHAPTER

➤ Version Control Basics

➤ What is Git

➤ Advantages of Git

➤ Disadvantages of Git

➤ History of Git

This book should hopefully be a comprehensive guide for learning all the essentials of Git for all the developers and learners out there. To begin with, in Chapter 1, we will be covering a fairly diverse set of topics, from the basic functioning of version control systems (VCSs), to an important and successful example of the software, Git, its history, advantages, as well as disadvantages. So, let's begin.

DOI: 10.1201/9781003229100-1

VERSION CONTROL BASICS

A version control is a kind of system which allows you to keep track of the changes that have been made to a code over a duration of time. Making use of version control comes with its advantages. A version control software will keep track of all the changes that have been made to a code in a special, specific database. This means that you can, at any given point in time, revert back to the older versions of the code you are working on. Consequently, it is easier to track the mistakes committed and rectify them while ensuring minimal disruption to your team members. Collaboration on the same code, therefore, become a significantly more manageable task.

Because coding is an essential part of the data sciences, it is recommended to make use of version control to ensure proper maintenance of the databases as well as the source code. All the changes made are recorded, and the proper streamlining of group projects significantly enhances their efficiency. Without a VCS, you and your team member are working on a shared folder and the same bunch of files. At some point in time, one individual is bound to overwrite the work of others. With a VCS, everyone can work freely, on any file at any given point in time. The software will eventually collate all the changes for a common version. One will never be confused as to where the latest version of a particular project is, it is always in your VCS.

Git happens to be one of the most popular VCSs. Not only that, Git is a distributed version control system (DVCS), i.e. a system of peer-to-peer version control, unlike centralized systems like Subversion (SVN). In Git, the changes made are not stored in one central repository. This will be a very complicated process, since every individual working on a specific project not only has to have access to the central repository, but also has to download the latest version of a specific project in order to be able to make changes to it. Git instead gives everyone a localized repository with its own specific history. So, Git is this fairly simple and efficient tool that facilitates version control in collaboration with affiliated services like GitHub, a Git repository hosting service which also provides access control and various task management tools for projects.

Version control is also variably referred to as source control. It has now become a very crucial aspect of high-performing development, since, with the acceleration of development environments, version control softwares help teams work faster and smarter. VCS also ensures a significant increase in successful deployments as well as a reduction in development time, making them especially useful for DevOps teams, who are responsible for combining software development with IT operations.

A source code is of critical importance for any and every software project. It is a precious asset containing knowledge about the problem at hand that the developers have collected and collated through tremendous effort. A VCS protects the source code from a potential catastrophe as well as the vagaries of human error. Software developers, often working in teams, are always in the process of writing new source code as well as making changes to the pre-existing source code. The code for a particular project or app software is usually arranged in the form of a folder, also referred to as a "file tree". One developer may be writing a new source code, while another is fixing an unrelated bug by making modifications to the existing source code. A good VCS will ensure that this concurrent work does not conflict with each other. Changes being made in one part of the software will inevitably be incompatible with the work done by another coder in a different part of the software. These issues have to be discovered and resolved without hindering the development being made by the rest of the team. Additionally, any change being made to the code may lead to the rise of more bugs. A code needs to perpetually be tested; a good VCS ensures that the development and testing go on smoothly till a new code is created.

Further, a good VCS should work on any platform rather than prescribing the Operating System a coder must use. It is important to support a developer's preferred workflow instead of imposing a specific methodology of working. Without VCS, a software development team is bound to run into problems like a set of incompatible changes incorporated that then have to be separately, and painstakingly, figured out and reworked. The powerful advantages of a VCS are further magnified as software development teams scale up to include more coders, wherein a VCS plays an indispensable role in preserving the efficiency, speed, and agility of the teams.

VCSs are of two types: Source Code Management (SCM) tools and Revision Control System (RCS). RCSs work well as standalone applications. Applications like word processors or spreadsheets have various mechanisms for control. There are numerous unique features of VCSs—the user is provided with an updated history for various types of files, no other repository system is needed, the repository can be cloned depending on the needs and availability of the team members. The last feature, in particular, can be a life-saver in case of system failures or accidental deletions. Further, VCS usually comes with a tag system that can help the user to differentiate between alpha, beta, or numerous other release versions for multiple documents.

Regardless of the kind of VCS one is working with, they offer the crucial facility of traceability. Every change made can not only be tracked, but also annotated to highlight the purpose and intent of the coder and its connection to the larger project. This allows the coders to make suitable changes that are in accordance with the long-term design of a specific system. This is of particular help while working on legacy codes, since it helps the developers assess the amount of future work needed with a fair degree of accuracy.

VCSs can also be subdivided into three kinds:

1. **Local VCS:** Local VCS keeps track of files within the local system. This approach is commonly used and simple, but also prone to errors, since the odds of writing into the wrong file are higher.

2. **Centralized VCSs:** Here, all the changes made to the file are kept track of by the centralized server. The centralized server contains all the information on the numerous versions of the main files, along with the list of clients who have access to the files. TortoiseSVN, a SVN client, which is implemented as a Microsoft Windows shell extension, to help programmers in managing the different versions of the source code for their programs, is a good example of centralized VCS.

3. **DVCS:** DVCS was developed in order to overcome the limitations of the centralized VCS. The clients are allowed to completely replicate the repository as well as its full history. In case a server dies, any of the client repositories should be copied to the server in order to resuscitate it. Every single clone contains a full backup of all the data. Git is a popular and highly successful example of DVCS.

While it is certainly possible to work on projects without VCS, these systems have become so ubiquitous that doing so would involve a professional risk that no development team will be willing to take. The moot question then is not if we should use a VCS, but what kind of VCS should one use. Different kinds of VCSs available for software development teams are Git, Mercurial, SVN, Concurrent Version System (CVS), etc. Mercurial is a freely available SCM tool that can handle projects of varying complexity, with its easy to handle and intuitive interface. While CVS works on distributed application structure for software development, SVN is a free VCS by CollabNet which can store and manage your TestComplete test projects as well as project suites.

There are some handy tips and tricks you can use for smooth functioning while working with VCS, whether it is the centralized VCS or the DVCS.

- Write a good, descriptive commit message. This is useful especially when someone is examining a change, and can therefore understand the purpose and intent of the change, if you convey the same with clarity. When someone is examining changes related to a concept, they are bound to look through the commit messages. Commits are elementary units for working in Git. Without commits, you will be unable to share your work with others.

- Ensure that each commit has a single purpose and that it only focuses on implementing that purpose. The purpose of version history is rendered redundant if a single commit contains code for multiple purposes, or if code for a specific purpose is spread across multiple commits.

- Avoid indiscriminate commits and always ensure that you provide specific files to commit. Whenever committing changes, you must make sure that you have not committed more than you intended to.

- Incorporate the changes other team members have made, and ensure that you are working on the most up-to-date version of the main file. If you do so, you are avoiding potential conflicts and incompatibilities that are certain to come if two commands go against each other.

- In a similar vein as the last point, make sure you share the changes you have made as soon as possible with your colleagues, before you go on to make other, unrelated changes to the main file. Basically, establish a coordination routine with your fellow team members to ensure the minimization of conflicting situations. For these purposes, Git provides the option of creating a Bare Git repository. In Git, a repository can be created using the git init command as well as the git init—bare command. Repositories created using the former are called working directories, while the ones created using the latter are known as bare repos. Bares Repos and Working Directories are structurally different. While the latter is used for work, the former is only meant to be shared with fellow developers at a centralized place where everyone can record their changes. Since Git is a DVCS, no one can directly edit the file in the shared central repository. So the coders instead can clone the shared bare repo and make the necessary changes within their working copies, and later they make changes made available to their team members. Since a shared bare repo will not be edited, it does not have a working tree.

- Do not use very long lines, keep the limit of each sentence to 80 characters. With long lines, there are chances that multiple edits will fall within the same line and subsequently conflict with one another. Also, do not refill or rejustify the paragraphs. It changes every line of the paragraph, making it harder to determine what changes were made in a particular commit.

- Do not commit generated files to version control. VCS is meant for files that are supposed to be edited. For example, you must not commit .pdf files which have been generated from a text formatting application. However, you can commit the source files from which the .pdf files have been generated.

- Understand and learn about your merge tools. You are likely to create conflicts if you are having a bad mental health day, are stressed out due to an upcoming deadline, etc. To handle these circumstances, become well versed with your Merge tool.

- Never forget to obtain and store your own copy of the project file, also referred to as "cloning" or "checking out".

WHAT IS GIT?

Git is a version control software meant for tracking changes in a given set of files, for ensuring coordinated work among programmers who are collaboratively developing a source code for software development. Its proposed goals are speed, support for distributed, non-linear workflows, as well as data integrity. To quote its original author, Linus Torvalds, "You can do a lot of things with Git, and many of the rules of what you *should* do are not so much technical limitations but are about what works well when working together with other people. So Git is a very powerful set of tools" (Torvalds, 2015).

Git is a free plus open-source software distributed under the GNU General Public License version 2. Apart from version control, Git is also used for other applications including content management as well as configuration management. The creator of the operating system Linux, Linus Torvalds, developed and launched Git in 2005. He took up this project because all the open-source VCSs available at that time were failing to match the requirements of the Linux kernel development. Basically, the relationship between the VCS BitKeeper and the Linux team had broken. Some kernel developers also made significant contributions to Git's early development. Junio Hamano has been responsible for the core development and maintenance of the system since 2005. Each and every Git directory on every system is an absolute repository with a full-fledged history and powerful abilities of tracking versions of the central code, irrespective of a central server or access to networks. This is unlike most client-server systems, but a feature that is shared by other DVCSs. It is important to note how Git records change. While CVSs store the changes made to a file over a period of time, Git merely stores the snapshot of the changed file. This means that if a file has not changed between two versions, Git will not copy it again and will simply retain the reference of the original file. This also ensures memory optimization within the system.

Git has a small footprint, high speed, and is easy to learn. Its salient features include providing a convenient staging area, ensuring space for multiple workflows, as well as provision for cheap local branching. Understanding the fundamentals of Git is very important if you intend to use it for work purposes in the future. If you are familiar with other kinds of VCSs, particularly centralized VCSs, it is better to keep that information aside while studying Git to avoid any unnecessary confusion. Even though Git's user interface seems similar to that of other VCSs, Git stores and processes information in a significantly different fashion.

In Git, most operations require only local resources and files for purposes of operation. Due to this, Git has a tremendously high speed, as the entire history of the project is on your local disk, making the operations nearly instantaneous. This further implies that as a coder, you can do almost everything on Git, even if you are offline. There is no conception of a master or central repository with Git. The Git repository on your system is self-contained and requires no other server. It contains information on all the branches, commits, tags, everything. If your VPN client is not working properly, it doesn't matter. You can still work. This liberty is practically impossible for other systems. SVN and CVS allow you to edit files, but you cannot commit changes to your database if you're offline, since the database itself is online. Perforce also cannot be operated offline.

Also, in GitHub, all data fed is checksummed before storage, and is subsequently referred to using that checksum, making it impossible to create changes in the file without Git coming to know of them. This happens to be one of the core features of Git and is integrated into the system at the minutest levels. If you lose information in transit, or if a file gets corrupted, Git will be able to detect it. The name of the mechanism that Git makes use of for checksumming is called SHA-1 hash. It is a 40 character string that is composed of hexadecimal characters which are calculated using either the contents of a particular file, or the directory structure of Git. You should see hash values a lot in Git since it makes extensive use of them. So much so that Git stores everything in its database not with file names, but utilizing the hash value of its contents.

With Git, you can also push and pull changes from other Git repositories. Those repositories could be anywhere, your own file system, that of a colleague, or even a distant server. So, you can make changes in your own repository, fetch changes incorporated by other team members, and consequently, merge the data as many times as is needed.

This means that you can work in isolation, but also synchronize the data easily with the rest of your team. Push and Pull features are exceptions to all the other operations on Git that are carried out locally. Not only that, the centralized approach of systems like SVN too can be replicated on Git using platforms like GitHub, GitLab, Bitbucket, etc.

Git just adds data. Any action you do on Git basically only adds more data to the Git repository. The system ensures you cannot erase data or do anything that cannot be undone. You will of course lose changes if you do not commit them properly, but once you have committed data into a snapshot in Git, it is unlikely that you will lose it, particularly if you continue pushing your database into another repository. So, Git offers you a safe space to experiment without the fear of screwing up things too dramatically.

Git offers a few basic tools to undo the changes you have made. However, be mindful that you cannot undo some of the undos themselves. This is a space where you may end up losing work if you mismanage. A common undo that is used often is if you mess up your commit message or commit too early, without adding the necessary files. To redo that particular commit, make the additional changes you forgot about, stage them, and recommit using the amend option. From Git version 2.23.0, the command git restore, an alternative to git reset, can also be used for purposes of undoing changes.

Git is not a SCM tool, as per its initial design approach. Nevertheless, its features being created as needed, Git has now developed a set of characteristics that can be expected out of a traditional SCM system. Git utilizes two data structures, a mutable index, also referred to as a stage or cache, that caches information regarding the working directory, as well as an append-only object database, which is immutable and contains the next revision to be committed. You will encounter five different objects within the object database:

1. **Blob:** It is the content of a file. Blobs do not have timestamps, or even a proper file name. In Git, each blob is a version of the file, and contains that particular file's data.

2. **Tree Object:** A directory containing the list of file names.

3. **Commit Object:** It contains the name of a tree object, a log message, a timestamp, as well as the names of parent commit objects. It basically acts as a link between the tree objects in history.

4. **Tag:** Contains metadata related to another object. It is most commonly used to store a digital signature of a commit object.

5. **Packfile:** A compressed Zlib version of multiple other objects. Advantages of use include ease of transportation through network protocols as well as the compactness provided.

Every object in Git is identified using the SHA-1 hash of its contents. Git computes the hash value and utilizes it for naming the object. Every object is put into a directory using the first two characters of its hash. The remaining hash is used as a file name for the object. Further, to show the locations of various commits, Git stores labels called refs, short for references.

Another important thing to learn about Git, it has three main states that contain your files, Modified, Staged, and Committed. Modified implies you have made changes to the file but are yet to commit those changes to your database. A staged state is when you mark a modified version of the file to go to your next commit snapshot. Committed implies that the data has been safely secured into the database.

Parallelly, there are also three central sections of any Git project—the working tree, the staging area, and the Git directory. The working tree is a checkout of a version of the project. The files are pulled directly from the compressed database of the Git directory, and placed on your disk for you to conduct the necessary edits. The staging area, also known as the "index", is a file in the Git directory storing the information that will go into your next commit. Remember that the staging area is a place to assemble your commits and save the snapshots of all the work you have done so far. You are allowed to choose the files as well as the lines that are to be a part of your next commit, allowing you to manufacture commits relevant to the work that you are doing. Adding certain files to the staging area is only preparing yourself for the next commit, and not the actual act of committing, for which you need to use the git commit command. Once a commit is created, it will move to the repository, rendering the staging area vacant. Once a commit is created, even if the entire working tree happens to get deleted and even if the staging area has been cleared, your content can still be recovered. The Git directory stores the object database and the metadata for your project. It is the most important aspect of Git. The directory is what gets copied when you clone a repository from another system.

So an elementary Git workflow will follow the following steps:

- You will modify the files in the working tree.

- The changes you want to make in your next commit have to be selectively staged.

- You commit, taking the files from the staging area, and storing their snapshot permanently in the Git directory.

All in all, a particular version of the file will be considered committed if it has been saved within the Git directory. It is considered staged if it has been modified and sent to the staging area. And if has been changed since checkout but is yet to be staged, it will be considered modified. Commits are the stable snapshots stored within the Git repository. Git shall never modify the contents of a commit unless, of course, you explicitly ask it to do so.

ADVANTAGES OF GIT

Moving from a centralized VCS to Git will fundamentally change the way your coders create software. If your organization is heavily reliant on software for critical applications, the altered workflow is bound to impact the entire business. Hopefully, Git should benefit each and every aspect of your organization, whether it is marketing or development. Some of the benefits that Git provides to coders are speed, simplicity, proper distribution, a conducive environment for parallel development with the support of hundreds of branches, as well as integrity. Git, therefore, is necessary not just for effective software development, but also for conducting business with efficiency and agility.

For Development

Git's branching capabilities happen to be one of its most advantageous features. Unlike the branches of centralized VCSs, Git branches are cheap and easier to merge. This provides the facility of feature branch workflow, which can significantly benefit an organization. Every change to the code base is provided in an isolated environment. The main branch contains the production quality code, and any change, big or small, consequently has to be committed to a new branch. Your development work is thus represented with as much focus as your backlog. A Jira ticket, for example, can be addressed using its own feature branch.

Being a DVCS, Git provides better speed. Everyone can work on their own changes separately in their local repositories without any threat of blocking and intermittent interruptions. If a developer accidentally eliminates her/his own repository, they can simply clone someone else's and start anew. This makes sure that Git is resilient to crashes since each node (a system on which a single developer works) has a copy of the source tree. Apart from this, the issues of security are effectively handled by Git with the cryptographic method SHA-1, an algorithm responsible for managing your versions, directory, and files, to make sure that your work is not corrupted.

SCM tools like Bitbucket further enhance Git's core functionality with facilities like pull requests. A developer can ask another to merge their branch in their own repository, allowing them to keep track of changes committed. This also helps in initiating deliberations on the work done before committing it to the main codebase. Junior developers can also utilize pull requests as formal code reviews to make sure that they are not botching up the entire project.

Git is highly popular among open-source projects, making it easy to leverage third parties as well as encouraging them to fork their own open-source code. Today, a formidable number of projects, both personal as well as commercial, make use of Git for purposes of version control. If you are using Git, you will not have to train new hires since they will probably already be familiar with the system.

Git facilitates a faster release cycle as well as an agile workflow, wherein smaller changes are shared more frequently by team members. So, naturally, Git works very well with fast delivery environments, allowing you to automate deployment as per your wants and needs.

Git for Marketing

Git can fundamentally change a traditional development workflow for marketing, wherein a centralized VCS would roll up all the changes committed into a single release. A shorter development cycle allows Git to synchronize multiple activities with separate releases.

Git for Product Management

The features utilized here are similar to the ones incorporated for purposes of marketing. The frequent releases will naturally imply more customer feedback as well as updates that will have to be incorporated in response to that feedback.

With Git, you can push out a solution for your customers as soon as your developers have resolved the issue with code changes. If your priorities change and you have to wait before introducing a new feature, that particular branch can sit in waiting till your engineers come around to it.

Git for Designing

Git provides a healthy and safe atmosphere for your designers to experiment. Feature branches allow rapid prototyping, and allow the designers to observe how their changes will eventually look like in the working copy, without the threat of destroying the present functionality of the product. This also allows the designers to provide updates to other important stakeholders. Pull requests to help everyone involved to come aboard the iteration process. Working via branches also means that you can incorporate the changes, or not. There is no pressure to do either, and the UI developers can make sure that only their best, most well-thought-out ideas eventually reach their customers. Other features that are of particular help to the designers are:

- **Context Switching:** You can switch back and forth between commits, and codes, old and new.

- **Role-Based Code:** Multiple lines of functionality. A branch can go into production, while the other is still being tested.

- **Disposable Experimentation:** Try out new ideas and discard them, if found unviable, without affecting the functionality of the source code, and the product at large.

Git for Customer Support

If a customer is going through an issue, you can immediately provide a bug fix, instead of making them wait for your next monolithic version release. Your developers can patch the problem immediately, improving your customer satisfaction and ratings.

Git for HR

Using Git will encourage developers to join your organization, since employees are drawn to companies providing healthy opportunities for career growth and development, and leveraging Git is an advantage that any developer would like to have, whether your organization happens to be big or small.

Git for Budget Management

Efficiency is perhaps the most salient feature of Git. The organization does not lose man-hours spent on integrating changes in centralized VCS. The work of junior developers too is effectively utilized. Designers are allowed to test features on the product with significantly less overhead. The marketing team can avoid putting efforts in features that are unpopular, and customer complaints can be responded to promptly.

DISADVANTAGES OF GIT

Some of the disadvantages of making use of GIT are:

- Git is slow on Windows, and requires long and convoluted command lines for input. Further, it cannot keep track of renaming, and requires a high degree of technical knowledge from the developer. Commands like Git Rebase can also invalidate tests or change the chronology of commits, defying the very purpose of version history. Furthermore, code merging making use of the command line does not entail a straightforward process, particularly if there are conflicts involved. Needless to say, merging is a ripe location of disputes among developers. Creating open communication channels to deliberate on the merging process, before integrating all the modifications together should help in reducing conflicts. Commands, in general, can be confusing, simply because there are so many of them. For example, if you are a user moving from SVN to Git, and you need to find Git's equivalent of "svn revert", you have to make use of a specific kind of git checkout. Mercurial, a distributed revision control tool, on the other hand, has a fairly smaller, more comprehensible set of commands, enhancing the accessibility of the tool. Not only that, because the developer commits to the server in SVN, they take into account changes incorporated by one another sooner and not later, reducing the possibility of hard-to-resolve conflicts or disagreements, a possibility in Git because the developers work independently and sometimes end up deviating too far from each other's work.

- The Graphical User Interface (GUI) is not effective and difficult to maneuver through. Git also has poor usability ratings, and makes use of a large amount of resources, slowing down the user's performance.

- It is important that the central service sets up multiple package repositories for each and every project. This is because Git does not provide support for checking out sub-trees. Furthermore, it is very difficult to merge without committing. This leads to a fairly large number of small commits, making the repository history very complex and difficult to read. Commits can be combined using Git Rebase, but that too is a very complex process that the developers must first learn and understand properly.

- Git cannot keep track of empty folders and suffers due to a lack of Windows support.

- Multiple branches are needed to support the parallel development being conducted by coding teams. The overall data model is highly complex with index, local, and remote repositories, working copies, etc. Also, Git works with an exclusive set of jargon words whose meaning is not what it explicitly seems; terms like ref, remote, index, refspec, origin, tracking branches, stash, pull, staging, rebase, revert, reset, reflog, and so many others, need to be learnt about properly to work on Git with a fair degree of agility. These issues make the learning process slower and more difficult, especially for inexperienced developers trying to get up to speed. To make rapid and effective use of Git repositories, a developer should know basic programming languages like Hypertext Markup Language (HTML), JavaScript, Cascading Style Sheets (CSS), etc. You must also be familiar with working on open-source applications and other platforms. Technical

know-how on other aspects of work that a programmer must be well-versed with include:

- Knowledge of how one can back up the work
  on the servers as well as platforms available like
  GitHub.

- A basic as well as high-level comprehension of
  Git commands to work around the Git repos with
  efficiency.

- How one can set up and install Git on different
  kinds of Operating Systems, along with being
  well-versed vis-à-vis the Git workflow, from creating a new repo, deleting an old one, as well as
  merging two repos, to the cloning of a repo, raising a pull request, and other commands.

- Git cannot support binary files. It drags and its speed
  is dramatically reduced if files containing non-text
  information are to be used often. Git also lacks in-
  built access control, as well as access control mechanisms for purposes of security. The process of packing
  too is immensely costly. Its performance is recognized as poor for files containing a large amount of
  data. Mercurial, another source control management
  (SCM) tool, works significantly better on repositories
  containing a number of multi-megabyte files.

Apart from these factors, transitioning to Git isn't considered particularly necessary for products where the
focus is primarily on maintenance, i.e. the development
aspect is minimal and innovation is, for all practical purposes, absent. Git is also not efficient when it comes to

maintaining a large number of files. Due to its complexity, it has a high level of error-proneness, so the IT administrators of an organization must carefully plan the architecture as well as the hierarchy of GIT transition. Along with this, developers should be able to make use of source control without getting bogged down with confusion.

Unlike Perforce and other systems, Git does not allow you to tag, branch, or clone only a part of the repository. You must branch/tag the whole repository. So, if you are working on multiple projects, which many do, you must keep track of multiple Git repositories. This makes files hard to find, despite the obvious improvements it makes to the performance of the team members. Additionally, transitioning massive SVN projects to Git can become an arduous task. And some projects require developers to work on common parts. This is what has led to the introduction of the concept of the submodule, which has its own set of command-line switches as well as operations.

Git also delves into the status of a remote server only if specifically asked to do so. This leads to issues. Git log shows you the work being done locally, as well as the work done by other team members before the last pull took place. It is not possible for you to be aware of what exactly is going on the remote server unless you make use of non-Git tools like GitHub. The absence of up-to-date information from the remote repository also leads to the problem of incorrect messaging. The code might inform you that your branch is up-to-date with the latest information, but it is most probably a lie. Git will not come to know if and when you have fallen behind unless it is explicitly asked to seek out that information from the remote repository. This is misleading though not a design flaw per se. Not seeking out information from the remote server is what is behind the superior performance and speed of Git. Git also is not restricted from modifying and browsing the central repository. Furthermore, it primarily works only on the Linux and the Unix platforms. Git VCS is certainly suitable for the developers working on open-source projects. However, the likelihood of too many versions, as well as practically unlimited rights of management to team members, creates a risk of asset loss, which is bound to hamper the company's project management. Due to this lack of a strategy to manage permissions, anybody with an account can import or export code, delete branches, perform rollback operations, etc. The utilization of script tools for the purposes of defining permissions can strongly help in mitigating the effects of this problem.

In the case of SVN, except in case of grid failures, data incorporated in the server is fairly secure. However, Git here faces a few issues. If you do not remember to push your stuff, it is very likely that you will lose it. Local folders can get deleted or overwritten. Additionally, even the changes that have been made and committed sometimes might not be safe. Deletion of Git branches might make certain commits inaccessible, since they stop belonging to the history of any particular branch. Commits of this kind will get quickly deleted, leading to you losing your work. Not only that, because of issues of network latency, sometimes the speed of accessing remote repositories is dramatically reduced on Git.

It is also possible to end up working on the wrong area in Git, especially if you forget to conduct the checkout command, and subsequently forget that you had left the repository in a branch. In the case of SVN, you can clearly see all the files, making it apparent which part you were earlier working on, significantly reducing the chances of this error being committed.

So, all in all, an arena where Git can potentially improve is widely recognized to be user-friendliness. Despite it being generally recognized as a useful solution for many software development life cycle problems, it has its own share of limitations. In comparison to Mercurial, for example, Git has a way steeper learning curve, with a significant duration of time required for people to understand the ins and outs of how Git stores and manipulates version history. The lack of intuition of its instructions has been pointed out by many. This is the reason behind why a significant number of commercial products seem to be filling the lacunae of Git. Vendors tend to incorporate unified hook management, incorporating layers of access control, as well as other convenient features to their Git version control project. These tools facilitate the members of the development teams, engineers, etc. to safely interact with Git and its many features.

Basically, if you have a strong requirement for a single, master copy of the code for your organization, you are recommended to use SVN. However, if you just intend to maintain parallel, but shared different customizations of the same product, go for Git. Git is an effective tool for the purposes it was originally designed for, the distributed development of open-source projects. However, due to significant complexity as well as the introduction of a plethora of new operations and concepts, Git will not be suitable for all projects, and a centralized source control system might do a better job for some specific projects. Your choice of VCS, therefore, should be made keeping in mind the nature of projects you/your organization generally handles.

HISTORY OF GIT

The development of Git began due to a creative conflict. It was during the early years of Linux kernel maintenance, i.e. from 1991 to 2002 that the software changes were passed around as archived files as well as patches. Eventually, in 2002, the Linux kernel project started using a proprietary DVCS which was called BitKeeper. BitKeeper was a proprietary, paid-for tool even at that point of time, but the Linux development community was allowed to use it free of cost. However, in 2005, the relationship between the Linux kernel community and the commercial company responsible for the development and maintenance of BitKeeper went sour, and the tool's free-of-cost status, subsequently was revoked. The man who was the copyright holder of BitKeeper, Larry McVoy, withdrew the free use of the product after his claim that Andrew Tridgell had created SourcePuller by making use of reverse engineering processes on the BitKeeper's protocols. This same incident was also responsible for spurring the creation of another VCS, Mercurial. McVoy's accusations led the Linux development community, particularly Linux creator Linus Torvalds, to build a tool of their own, utilizing their learnings and experiences with BitKeeper. Torvalds called the system "Git" because he liked the word, when he came across it in a Beatles song I'm So Tired (verse two). He says,

"The in-joke was that I name all my projects after myself, and this one was named 'Git.' Git is British slang for 'stupid person'.... There's a made-up acronym for it, too—Global Information Tracker—but that's really a 'backronym,' [something] made up after the fact" (Favell, 2020).

When the development is primarily being done by an in-house coding team, and has to be well managed and controlled, a centralized VCS should work perfectly decently. However, if there are hundreds or thousands of developers involved in a project, working remotely, independently, and voluntarily, with a high degree of experimentation involved, as it was in the case of projects like Linux, DVCS, then embodied by BitKeeper was way more ideal. Git, Monotone, and Mercurial, ultimately were modeled after the achievements of BitKeeper. To quote Torvalds, "BK was the big conceptual influence for the usage model, and really should get all the credit. For various reasons, I wanted to make the Git implementation and logic completely different from BK, but the conceptual notion of 'distributed VCS' really was the number one goal, and BK taught me the importance of that...Being truly distributed means forks are non-issues, and anybody can fork a project and do their own development, and then come back a month or a year later and say, 'Look at this great thing I've done'" (Favell, 2020).

A recurrent issue with the Client-Server VCSs also was that whoever hosted the main repository on their server also was the "owner" of the source code. The innovation of DVCSs resolved this problem. Now, there was no centralized repository under an individual's ownership, just a lot of clones that the developers could independently work on.

In the absence of a central "master" location, anyone could become a host and carry out their own development, which would later have to be merged. Merging the peripheral branches to the central repository was also a space riddled with its own set of problems. The use of cryptographic hash, a unique number for identification, to index every object, proved to be a major innovation here. While the use of hashes was not started by Git, the VCS did take it to a new level, wherein hashes were not merely utilized to identify newer versions of the elements of the file, but also how those versions were related to each other, with regard to the commits made, the larger tree, etc. With the use of the command "git diff", Git could successfully identify all the committed changes between the source code and the newer versions of the file, or even whole trees, by looking through the indexes of the hashes. This process also ends up becoming an intermediate step before performing merges, as it allows you to incrementally resolve the conflicts that will arise. The innovation of staging area, to conduct a comparison of different versions, as well as resolve the issues being encountered between the source code and additions made, before performing the merge, was revolutionary, though it was not immediately accepted by the developers used to other VCSs.

So, some of the goals that the developers had in mind were—the role of distribution, good ability in handling huge projects like the Linux kernel with a fair degree of efficiency and agility, particularly vis-à-vis the speed as well as the data size of the files, a simple design, providing a strong platform for non-linear development, i.e. the capacity to maintain thousands of parallel branches at the same time, speed, etc. As a design criterion, Torvalds specified that patching must not take more than three seconds. Further, he kept the example of Concurrent Versions Systems, i.e. CVSs in mind as to what not to do for his own DVCS. The workflow intended was modeled after BitKeeper, along with safeguards against threats of corruption, whether it be malicious or accidental. Ultimately, Git was launched, and the first merge of multiple branches on it occurred on April 18, 2005. Torvalds was able to achieve the performance goals he had in mind; on April 29, early Git successfully benchmarked recording patches to Linux kernel tree at the speed of 6.7 patches per second.

However, it was also important to appoint a maintainer for the newly created VCS. After writing Git, Torvalds gave it to the open-source community for reviews and contributions. On July 26, 2005, Torvalds handed over the responsibility of the maintenance of the project to Junio Hamano, a major contributor who remains the core maintainer of Git to this date. Hamano's innovations turned out to be so influential that after only a few months of Git's launch, Torvalds was able to take a step back and concentrate on Linux again, passing the responsibility of the maintenance of Git to Hamano. For Torvalds, "He had that obvious and all-important but hard-to-describe 'good taste' when it came to code and features...Junio really should get pretty much all the credit for Git—I started it, and I'll take credit for the design, but as a project, Junio is the person who has maintained it and made it be such a pleasant tool to use." Hamano still controls the larger direction of Git as a software, and is the final word on the changes made to the code, apart from holding the record for most commits (Favell, 2020).

Other important contributors during the early development of Git were Jeff King, Shawn Pearce, and Johannes Schindelin. They started out as volunteers, and are now employed full-time by companies that rely on Git to conduct their daily operations, and therefore make investments to ensure its upkeep and improvement. Jeff King, also known as Peff, started making contributions as a student. He did his first commit in 2006, when he spotted and fixed a bug in git-CSV import, while moving his repositories to Git from CVS. To quote King, "I was a graduate student in computer science at the time," he says, "so I spent a lot of time lurking on Git's mailing list, answering questions and fixing bugs—sometimes things that bothered me, sometimes in response to other people's reports. By around 2008, I had become one of the main contributors, quite by accident" (Favell, 2020). King has since been employed by GitHub, and now works for the website, apart from making additional contributions to Git.

Shawn Pearce too did exemplary work on JGit, which was responsible for opening up Git to the Android and Java ecosystems, while Johannes Schindelin worked on Git for Windows, which subsequently opened up the Windows community to Git. Later, they ended up working at Google and Microsoft, respectively.

Since its conception in 2005, Git has undergone a variety of changes, but has managed to retain the initial qualities it was supposed to embody according to its developers. The DVCS remains highly popular among coders and engineers, because it is incredibly fast, very efficient even in case of fairly huge projects, along with providing a spacious environment for branching and non-linear development.

We should now examine the reasons responsible for the wild success of Git, the undisputed leader of a highly competitive field. Today, world over, a large number of startups, multinationals, and collectives, including Google, Microsoft, and others, make use of Git to maintain source codes of their software projects. Many host their own Git projects, others utilize Git through its commercial hosting companies like GitHub, founded in 2007, GitLab, founded in 2011, as well as Bitbucket, founded in 2010. GitHub, the largest among the three of them, has 40 million developers attached to it, and was acquired in 2018 by Microsoft for a huge sum of $7.5 billion. While an aspect of its obvious appeal is that like Linux and Android, it is open source, there are other VCSs that happen to be open-source, like SVN, Mercurial, Monotone, CVS, etc. so being open-source alone cannot explain Git's emergence and ascendancy. Git's dominance over the market can be best demonstrated by a 2018 survey of developers by question and answer website Stack Overflow, where they enquired into the VCS choices of over 74,000 respondents. Git emerged as a clear numero uno, with over 88% mentioning it as their mode of conducting their daily programming operations. The very distant competitors were SVN, with 16.6% penetration, Team Foundation Version Control (11.3%), and Mercurial (3.7%). These results were so dramatic that Stack Overflow did not even bother asking the same question in its 2019 edition of the same survey. Git, of course, was the fastest DVCS, and remains so. With Git, once developers learnt the use of features available at the given speed, it became virtually impossible to go back to a slower software. Switching from one branch to another was fast, so was creating a

whole new branch. Merging branches too was an operation speedily conducted, only depending on the number of
changed files. Mercurial was a potential competitor, but it
was significantly slower and did not provide any extra features over Git. Initially, some preferred Mercurial because
it could, unlike Git, run natively on Windows. However,
the later versions of Git have worked upon this limitation,
with Windows now providing native binary support to Git
as well. Further, Mercurial stored branches, bookmarks,
unnamed branches, etc. in its repository. Git refers to all
these just as a branch. So, even in order to perform the first
commit, you must be able to select good branch names in
Mercurial, since they will get stored in the repository along
with your commits later on. In Git, a branch name is only
the location of present work, and not a part of the commit
data which will eventually be stored in DAG.

Furthermore, Git always allowed making changes to
the DAG even after the commit had been already performed. This allowed for the rewriting of the history of a
branch, ensuring a better, more readable version history
for the project. This was done by allowing commands
like "git rebase -i" and for more significant changes, "git
filter-branch".

Historically, a number of major open-source projects
switched to Git the years after its high-profile launch in
2005. So, it got a significant number of high-profile influ-
encers early on in its development. Keith Packard famously
chose Git for the X Window System in 2007. In his article
"Repository Formats Matter," he wrote, "I know Git suffers from its association with the wild and wooly kernel
developers, but they've pushed this tool to the limits and

it continues to shine. Right now, there's nothing even close in performance, reliability and functionality...Small incremental changes have been made which make the tools more consistent, and I hope to see those discussions continue" (Packard, 2007). Packard's decision for the X project proved influential, and several other projects came to similar conclusions regarding the utility of Git independently. However, the project hosting sites such as Google Code and SourceForge refrained from supporting Git in its early years despite some interest from the developers. The absent functionality of Git opened the doors for the launch of GitHub in early 2008. The subsequent social interactions facilitated by GitHub, the variety of developer support tools like fork, milestones, like, report issue, etc. further fueled the growth prospects of Git, making it highly viable for developers, young and old alike. Git also came out 14 years after the initial release of the Linux kernel, the UNIX-like OS, which meant that at the time of its release, Linus was significantly famous and well-known, so the VCS created too became popular fairly easily.

In this chapter, we learnt the basics of VCS software, preliminary details on Linus Torvalds-created Git, the history of the system, as well as its advantages and disadvantages. In the next chapter, we move to the installation of the software, what to do when you have to set it up for the first time, as well as the tips and troubleshooting involved in the same processes.

REFERENCES

Favell, A. (2020, February 4). The history of git: The road to domination. The History of Git: The Road to Domination. https://www.welcometothejungle.com/en/articles/btc-history-git.

Foundation, T. L. (2017, August 22). *10 years of Git: An interview with git creator Linus Torvalds*. Linux Foundation. Retrieved September 10, 2021, from https://www.linuxfoundation.org/blog/10-years-of-git-an-interview-with-git-creator-linus-torvalds/.

Packard, K. (2007). Repository Formats Matter. https://keithp.com/blogs/Repository_Formats_Matter/.

CHAPTER 2

The Basics

IN THIS CHAPTER

> ➤ Installing Git

> ➤ First Time Git Setup

> ➤ Tips and Troubleshooting

In the previous chapter, we covered a host of topics, including Version Control Basics, information on Git, its advantages, disadvantages, history, features, etc. In this chapter, we continue our journey with details on installation, first-time setup, as well as tips and troubleshooting tricks that can be used for Git. Read on to find out more.

INSTALLING GIT

Git can be easily installed on most of the operating systems like Linux, Mac, Windows, etc. Mostly, Git comes preinstalled on the Linux and Mac Machines. So you best first

DOI: 10.1201/9781003229100-2

check whether your system already contains Git, lest you reinstall it unnecessarily.

To check for Git, open your terminal application. On Mac, you should look for a command prompt application known as "Terminal". On Windows, open the Windows command prompt or "Git Bash". On opening the terminal application, type "git version". The output should tell you which version of Git is installed on your system, or it will let you know that "git" is a foreign command. If you get the latter result, you will have to install Git on your system manually.

Before being able to use Git, you must ensure that the latest version of the software is installed on your computer. You can install Git through another installer, through a package, or by downloading the source code, and then compiling it on your own. Installing GitHub Desktop should also install Git within your system if you already don't have it. GitHub Desktop will give you a command-line version of Git, alongside an effective Graphical User Interface (GUI). Whether you have Git installed or not, GitHub Desktop acts as a simple and efficient collaborative tool for Git. It will simplify your development workflow, allow you to add co-authors to your commits, see pull requests for your repositories as if it were from a local branch, permit syntax highlighting, etc.

If you wish to install Git on Linux through a binary installer, you should make use of the package management tool which comes alongside the distribution. If you use RPM-based distribution tools like Red Hat Enterprise Linux (RHEL), Community Enterprise Operating System (CentOS), or Fedora, make use of DNF. With Ubuntu or any other Debian-based distribution, use the command "apt". It is best to install Git on Linux with the preferred package manager of your system's Linux distribution. You can also build from source using tarballs, i.e. the tape archives used for opening as well as creating archive files on Linux and the other operating systems similar to Unix.

Several methods can potentially be adopted to install Git on a Mac. Apple tends to maintain their own fork of Git, but it usually falls behind the mainstream Git by many versions. The simplest way to go about your purpose is through the installation of the Xcode Command Line Tools. For Mavericks 10.9 and above, try running the command "git" from the Terminal. This should prompt you to install Git if you haven't done so already. Utilize a binary installer if you want the up-to-date version. You will also be able to find a Git installer for MacOS from the official Git website.

You can also install Git from Homebrew, which is an immensely popular package manager for Mac. To install Git on Homebrew, open a terminal window and use the command: "brew install git". Check that the command output has been completed, then verify the Git installation using the command "git version".

The official Git website is also the go-to place for installing Git on Windows. Visit the URL git-scm.com/download/win and your Git download should start automatically. Keep in mind that this is a project called Git for Windows, which is separate from Git. For an automated installation, you should utilize the community-maintained Git Chocolatey Package. Chocolatey packages usually install everything you need in order to maintain a piece of software into a single artifact, containing executable files, zips, scripts, wrapping installers, etc. into a complete compilation package file.

For Windows, you should also install Git extensions. Potential alternatives for Git extensions include TortoiseGit for the integration of Windows Explorer with Git, as well as Git Source Control Provider. Apart from this, you should also set up your Secure Shell (SSH) keys. The main purpose of SSH keys is that they link two systems with secure keys, which usually consist of numbers and letters to ensure secure communication. Git primarily uses SSH keys for internal communication. During work, whenever you will push to a remote repository or pull down from a private repository, you shall be making use of SSH. SSH keys are generally considered more secure than usernames as well as passwords. So, to interact with most repositories, you will have to generate an SSH, and that can be done using a tool called PuTTY. Your SSH keys will always come in pairs. You will have a private key (which you won't be able to see) as well as a public key which has to be pasted into the repositories that you have access to.

To acquire the latest version, it is recommended that you install Git from the source. Though Git has made significant progress in recent years, the fact remains that the binary installers still tend to lag behind. For installing Git from source, you must have access to the libraries Git is heavily dependent on; they are libiconv, expat, openssl, zlib, curl, and Autotools. If your system has DNF or apt-get, use them for installation with minimal dependencies.

With Debian-based distribution, you will be needing an install-info package. For RPM-based distribution, acquire the getopt package, usually preinstalled in distros that are based on Debian. With all the necessary dependencies, you should acquire the latest tarball from the official websites of Kernel or GitHub. The GitHub page usually provides more clarity on what the latest version is, though release signatures are available on Kernel pages as well.

Git is also accompanied by built-in GUI tools for committing as well as browsing. Depending on the platform-specific experiences you seek, there are a number of third-party tools available, like GitHub Desktop, SourceTree, TortoiseGit, Git Extensions, Magit, GitKraken, GitUp, Sublime Merge, Tower, SmartGit, Fugitive, Fork, gitg, GitAhead, GitEye, LazyGit, ungit, Guitar, Working Copy, Pocket Git, GitFox, gmaster, GitVine, and many, many others. If you have already installed Git, you should also be able to acquire the latest development versions from Git via the code:

```
git clone https://github.com/git/git
```

You can also go through the present contents of the Git repository through its web interface.

FIRST TIME GIT SET UP

Git is a type of free and open-source distributed version control system (VCS). It is also the most widely used modern VCS in today's world. Git works well on a wide variety of operating systems as well as Integrated Development Environments (IDEs). After installing Git on your system, there are a few things that you must do to customize the

Git environment according to your needs. You should have to perform these actions only once in a system, and they should stick through despite the upgrades. You can also alter these changes as and when you need by going through the commands again.

Git is enabled with a tool called "git config" which allows you to control the configuration variables, thus moderating various aspects of how Git operates and looks. These variables are generally stored in three places:

1. **[path]/etc/gitconfig file:** This file contains all the values for every user on the system as well as all the repositories. Since this is a system configuration file, you must have administrative privileges if you want to make changes to it.

2. **~/.gitconfig file:** It contains values specific to you, i.e. the user. The "global" option can make Git specifically read or write to this file, which consequently can affect all the repositories you use on your system. Once you have defined the ~/.gitconfig file, you are allowed to copy it to any other system where you use Git. This command will therefore ensure that you have the same identity as well as settings across all the systems that you use Git on.

3. **Config file in the Git directory:** This file is specific to a particular repository that you are currently using. The default "local" will make Git write to and read from this file. However, it is important that you are located in a Git Repository for this option to work well.

Moreover, the values of each level override the previous one. So, the values of .git/config will supersede those of [path]/etc/gitconfig, etc.

Establishing Your Identity

The most necessary thing to do after installing Git is setting your user name as well as password. This is because every commit you create will require this information, as well as contain it. As mentioned earlier, you will hopefully have to do it only once when you pass the "global" option, because Git will subsequently record it and conduct all the operations in your name on that system. If you need to change your name or email address for particular projects, you should run the command, but not the "global" option when you are working on that project. Several GUI tools will be able to help you to do this as and when you run them on your software.

Editing

After setting up your identity, you need to now go into the configuration details of the text editor that will be utilized whenever Git needs you to type up a message. Without your intervention, Git will end up using the default editor of your system. If you need to use a different text editor, say Emacs, do the following:

```
$ git config --global core. editor emacs
```

To use a different editor on Windows, you will have to type out the complete path leading up to its executable file. This too will vary depending on how your editor has been packaged.

Default Branch Name

Git will create a default branch called "master" as and when you create a new repository with "git init". From Git 2.28 onward, you can give a different name to the initial branch if you want to do so. To set "main" as the default branch name, you will need to do the following:

```
$ git config - -global init.defaultBranch
main
```

Check the Settings

If you want to go through all the configuration settings of your Git, utilize the "git config - -list" command, and your Git should be able to list out all the settings it can find at that point of time. You might sometimes see a few keys more than once. This is because Git ends up reading the same key from multiple sources. In cases of this kind, Git will make use of the last value it sees for every unique key. If you want to check what a particular key's value is according to Git, make use of the command "git config <key>". Because of reading a value from multiple files, it is possible that sometimes, you might get an unexpected value for a variable, and you cannot figure out the reasons for the same. If that happens, you can enquire Git on the "origin" of that value, and it should be able to tell you which file had the final say in determining the provided value.

Git also allows you to decide the colors for your console. The Linux OS users can make use of third-party Zsh configurators like *oh my zsh* in order to customize their terminal look with a variety of themes. The "color.ui" is the meta configuration that will include different color configurations available alongside your git commands. Apart from color.ui, there are several other granular color settings. Like color.ui, these color settings can be set to false, always, or auto. These color settings usually also have a particular color value set. Some of the examples of supported color values are normal, black, white, cyan (a mixture of green and blue), magenta, red, green, yellow, and blue. Colors might also be specified using ANSI 256 color values, hexadecimal color codes like #ff0000 if your terminal can facilitate it, etc.

Further, some softwares, like Apache Netbeans, also make use of badges and color coding to projects, folders, and package nodes, to inform the developer regarding the status of files contained within the local node. A blue badge, for example, denotes the presence of files that have been added, deleted, or modified, in the main working tree. This badge is also used to mark packages, but not the sub-packages. The badge also indicates changes within a particular item, for projects, folders, as well as subfolders. A red badge, on the other hand, contains files with conflicts. Like the blue badge, the marker is meant for packages, and not sub-packages. The badge is used to indicate the conflicts within a particular item, for the projects, folders, and subfolders.

Color coding, as mentioned above, is also utilized by Git to denote the current status of the files with regard to their repository. Black, i.e. no specific color means that the files have not undergone any changes. Blue means that the file has been modified locally. Green implies that a file has been locally added. Red implies the existence of an internal conflict. And gray indicates that the file has been ignored by Git, and therefore shall not be included in the versioning commands, i.e. Commit and Update. A file cannot be ignored if it is versioned.

There are other preliminary steps you must be familiar with in order to be able to work on Git. These are:

Creating a New Repo

You will have to use the git init command to create a new repo. git init is a one-time command that you are supposed to use during the new repo's initial setup. This command conceives a new .git subdirectory within your current operations directory. It is also used to create a new main branch. Let's assume that you have an existing project folder for which you have to create a new repo. So, to successfully conduct this operation, you must first cd the root project folder followed by the execution of the git init command. Pointing git init toward an existing project directory will further execute the initialization setup that has been mentioned above, but limited to that project directory only.

Git Clone

This will help in creating clones of an existing repository. If a particular project has already been set up in the Git central repository, the clone command should help the users in creating the local development clones for conducting their edits and commits. Cloning is a one-time operation, just like git init. Once a coder obtains her/his working copy, all the version control operations will subsequently be conducted locally. git clone creates copies of remote repositories. You give git clone a repository URL to work with. Git supports quite a few different network protocols as well as their corresponding URL formats. On the execution of this command, the latest version of the repo files on the remote servers shall be pulled down and included in a new folder. The new folder shall contain the complete history of the remote repository as well as the newly created branch.

Saving Changes

With the repository cloned, you can now begin committing the file version changes to it. After executing this action, your repo will have CommitTest.txt added to the history and will be tracking all the future updates to the file to maintain a proper record of the version history. Executing the git add—all command should also be able to take any changed or untracked files in the repo and subsequently add them for the purposes of updating the repo's working tree.

Git Push

Git Push plays an important role in ensuring Repo-to-repo collaboration. Git's understanding of a "working copy" is different from that of Subversion (SVN) wherein you checkout the code from a repository. Git does not discriminate between the working copies and the central repository, they are all to be considered full-fledged Git Repositories in and of themselves. So while the functioning of SVN is predicated on the relationship between the central repository and the working copies, the operations on Git, conversely, rely on how the repositories interact with each other. In Git, commits are to be pushed up and pulled down from one repository to other. Of course, you are allowed to give specific repositories special meaning.

For example, you could simply label a Git Repo as a "central repository" to replicate a centralized workflow on Git. However, functions of this kind have to be accomplished via conventions, and are not built-in into the VCS.

Bare and Cloned Repositories

Using the git clone command allows your repository to be configured for remote collaboration. Subsequently, if you make your changes and commit them, git push should be able to push those changes to your remote repositories. However, if you use git init in order to make a fresh repo, you will not have a remote repo to push your changes to. When initializing a new repo, you can go to a Git service like Bitbucket to create a repo there. You will acquire a Git URL which can then be added to your local Git repository and later git push to the hosted repository. After creating a remote repo, you will also need to update your local repository with proper mapping. If you wish to host your own remote repo, you will have to set up a "Bare Repository". This can be used to create a central but remote repository for Git.

Reverting Changes

To do away with the local changes made to specific files in the working tree as well as replacing the same files with the ones in the Index, do the following:

- Select a versioned file or folder, say from the Files, Favorites, or the Projects window.

- Go to Team > Revert Modifications from the central menu.

- Specify the additional options. (For example, choose whether to "Revert only Uncommitted Changes in Index to HEAD", "Revert all uncommitted changes in Working Tree and Index", or "Revert Uncommitted in the Working Tree to the State in Index")

- Click on the "Revert" button.

The IDE should now replace the selected files with the ones you have specified.

TIPS AND TROUBLESHOOTING

Git is a highly popular VCS widely used for a number of commercial as well as private development works. No matter how adept you might become at using this VCS, there are always new things to learn. The following tips and tricks should hopefully help you in operating the system with significant agility:

- **Autocorrection:** We all end up making typographical errors sometimes, but with Git's auto-correct feature enabled, you can allow it to automatically fix a mistyped command or subcommand. For example, for the purposes of checking the status, you make use of git status, but accidentally mistype it as "git stats". Normally, Git will simply inform you that the command you have used is not valid. For times when this becomes a recurrent issue, it is best for you to enable Git autocorrection within your Git configuration. If you wish to apply this configuration only for the repository you are working on currently, you should omit the—global option from your command.

The auto-correction feature should subsequently be enabled. Now, rather than suggesting the alternative, correct subcommand, Git will just run with the feature's top suggestion, which was git status in our example.

- **Counting commits:** During development, you might need to know the count of your commits for multiple reasons. The number of commits lets the developers know how a particular project is progressing, as well as the needs, if any, to increase the build number. Using the following command, counting your commits should be a fairly simple and straightforward process:

```
$ git rev-list - -count
```

Do make sure that the branch name you provide is a valid branch name from your current repository.

- **Repo optimization:** Your code repository is of immense value for your organization. Make habits of a few safe practices to ensure that your repository is clean, decently maintained, and updated. Make use of the .gitignore file. This ensures that Git won't store unwanted records like temporary files, binaries, etc. in your repository unnecessarily. Using the Git Garbage collection can also prove to be of significant value, especially if you and your team members make heavy use of push and pull commands. This command is an internal utility feature that cleans up inaccessible or "orphaned" git objects from your repositories.

- **Data backup:** While it is mostly okay to get rid of your untracked files; in some situations, you might also have to back them up in case you need them later. Git, along with Bash Command Piping, allows you to create a zip archive of your untracked files. The files listed in. gitignore however, are excluded.

- **Familiarize yourself with your .git folder:** Each repository has a special, hidden folder called the .git folder. While your working tree contains the state of files in your present checkout, it is the .git folder that contains the versioning information of the project files. Not only that, but this folder also contains all the references, repository data, configuration files, logs, information about the state of HEAD, etc. Deleting this folder will eliminate your project history, though your source code will survive. This implies that the local copy of your project is not under version control anymore. You will not be able to track your changes, or push/pull to/from a remote repository. The .git folder is managed by the Git software and mostly should not be messed around with. Nevertheless, you can look through the artifacts in the directory, whether it be the current state of the HEAD, or an available description of your repository. The Git Hooks folder will offer you examples of the hook files that can be read through to acquire an understanding of what is possible on Git via the use of Git hooks.

- **View the file of another branch:** Git also has commands available to view the contents of a file from another branch without actually having to switch your branch. For example, if you want to go through the contents of the file xyz on the main branch, execute the command:

```
$ git show main:xyz
```

Now, you would be able to view the contents of the file from your own terminal.

- **Conducting searches:** You can conduct searches on Git even if you are unsure about which commit, or branch, you made your changes to. This should save you plenty of time as well as boost your productivity.

Because Git is very efficient at helping small teams in managing their software development, keeping some tips in mind can make collaborative work even more effective. To make Git work well with diverse teams, with members having varying levels of expertise, keep the following tips in mind:

- **Formalize your Git conventions:** Make sure that your team has a standard set of conventions for coding, tagging, branch naming, etc. Every organization has its own set of good practices, and you should also be able to find recommendations from coders working in teams online. What is crucial is that a standardized set of rules is established right from the start and followed through by the entire team. This is also important because team members usually have a varying set of capacities, so maintaining a basic set of instructions for the common Git operations helps build a sense of cohesion and uniformity with regard to the project.

- **Merging changes:** Each team member will usually work on a separate feature branch. Despite that, some common files are modified by everyone. So while merging the changes to the master branch, the process will not be instant or automatic. Human intervention and even deliberation between team members will be a must to reconcile the different changes made to a file. So you will have to learn how to handle the various Git Merge techniques. Git has features for the editors to be able to resolve the merge conflicts. There are options to conduct a merge in each part of the file where they are needed. You can choose to keep your changes, the changes made by the other developers, or both if they are not mutually incompatible. You are advised to pick a different code editor if your Git doesn't provide you with these facilities.

- **Rebasing:** Rebase your feature branch against the master branch often. This should rewrite the history of your features branch. Doing so will make your features branch look like the master one, with all the updates of the master incorporated in it as well. Further, all the commits you made will be replayed at the top, and therefore will be appearing sequentially in the Git logs. There will be merge conflicts as you go along the way, but this is also the best way of resolving them, as it will only impact your features branch. So, fix the conflicts, perform the regression testing, then merge the feature branch back with the master, i.e. rebase and perform the merge. However, in the meantime, if someone else has pushed changes into the master branch that conflict with yours, the Git Merge will have problems again, which you will have to resolve, before repeating the regression testing all over again. This might take time, but it will make your commit history accessible as well as readable, containing a meaningful arrangement of features. If you do not rebase regularly, the history of the master branch will contain commits from a plethora of features that are being developed simultaneously. This kind of history is highly convoluted, and very difficult to read through. So the commit times are not that important as long as you have a history that can be easily reviewed.

- **Removing commits before merge:** When working on your node, you will obviously commit even if the changes in themselves are minor. However, if every feature branch is creating scores of commits, the total number for the master branch will become unnecessarily huge, as more features will be added later on. Ideally, only a few commits (go for a single-digit number) should be sent out for a single features branch. To do this, eliminate multiple commits into only a few by framing more complex messages. Basically, you will have to revise the commits, choose to pick or squash them. Picking implies retaining the commit in its original state, while squashing would imply choosing to merge a commit with one or two others. This will give you an opportunity to edit, clean up, improve clarity, as well as get rid of a few commits that retrospectively do not look too necessary and can be done away with, for example, a commit on fixing a typographical issue. Crucially, do not forget to update your remote feature branch, since your commit history has now been rewritten.

- **Using tags:** If you wish to preserve the present state of a branch to record a milestone or for any other reason, you are advised to make use of tags. While your branch is keeping a record of its history through commits, a tag is a snapshot of the state of the branch at the moment it is taken. So, a tag can be understood as a branch without history, or a pointer to a specific commit that was made immediately before the tag was taken.

  Configuration control entails preserving the different stages of a particular code so that those stages can be revisited, if needed, in the future. For example, a customer was provided with a software that corresponds to a tag that was created. Now, if the customer happens to report an issue with the system, you will have to reproduce that state of code to allow the developers to come up with a bug fix. But the code has evolved since that point of time, and the tag then can help you in resolving the matter at hand. Sometimes, the developed code might have automatically resolved the issue being faced by the customer, but obviously, it might not necessarily always be so. A tag will recreate the branch that you can then, work on. Apart from this, Git gives you the options to use annotated as well as signed tags, if you find that they can benefit your project.

- **Embedding:** The binary files created as part of the embedded projects have a fixed name. The file name, however, cannot lead you to the corresponding tag you need to revisit. So you must remember to embed the tag within the software during build time to be prepared to resolve any issues pertaining to it that might arise in the future. The process of embedding can be automated during the build process. Usually, the tag string generated by the command git describe is inserted within the code before conducting code compilation so that the resultant executable should be able to print the tag string when it is booting up. So, whenever a customer reports a particular issue, they are guided to send you the boot output, or one of its copies.

- **Editing commits:** Important to resolve typos. Use of—amend to create new and accurate commits. However, you cannot use this command for modifying commits that have already been pushed to the central repository.

  If you forgot to mention the name of a file while using Git Add, add it on later and use the amend option:

```
git add name_forgotten_file
git commit --amend
```

- **Pre-push cleaning:** Amend is the best option for editing your commits on Git. However, it cannot be used if the commit you intend to edit is not the last one you worked on. Rebasing comes to your rescue in situations of that kind. Rebasing also offers you other options apart from editing the commits. You are also allowed to delete, reorder, or squash the commits.

You can also remove a file from Git, without removing it from the file system. Sometimes, it is possible that you end up with a bunch of unnecessary files during the conduction of the git add command. In situations of this kind, use the git rm command to remove the said files from the staging area. The file will also be added to .gitignore so that the software does not make the same mistake again.

You must also have the technical know-how of reverting pushed commits. Despite amendments and rebasing, there will be instances when flawed commits will end up reaching your central repository. However, there are a set of git revert commands that allow you to revert commits with a specific ID, the second to last commit you worked on, and even multiple commits together. Of course, sometimes you might not want to create more revert commits, and only wish to apply changes to your working tree. For this, you can use the—*no-commit/-n* command option.

Git makes sure that you do not have to resolve repeated merge conflicts. Fixing merge conflicts is already a tiresome process. Say, you have to merge multiple feature branches together, and there is a range of conflicts. You resolve them and then realize that one of the branches is not prepared for the merge yet, so you must postpone the process. You will now merge at the due appointed hour, but because Git has recorded your resolutions, you will not have to work on the conflicts you previously resolved all over again.

In case you have to find a problematic commit after the merge has been completed, the process can be particularly difficult as well as time-consuming. For this, Git allows you to use a set of commands (git bisect commands) for dissecting a particular session, marking the current revision as bad, marking the last observable good revision, etc.

The tips and tricks mentioned above, if learnt, remembered, and utilized properly, should help you navigate the charted but difficult terrains of Git. Good Luck!

This chapter helped us in learning about how to install our Git for the first time, set it up properly, as well as the tips for troubleshooting and smooth functioning of the system. The next chapter will have us shifting our focus onto Git Repositories, how to record changes on them, working with remotes, the concepts of git aliases as well as tagging. Read on.

Working with Repositories

In the previous chapter, we were educated on the basics of Git, its installation, first-time setup, and the important tips to keep in mind for troubleshooting and properly conducted development work. Now, as we begin this chapter, we will shift our focus to Git Repositories, what they are, how they

DOI: 10.1201/9781003229100-3

record changes, how we can work with Remotes, concepts like Git Aliases as well as Tagging. Read on to learn more!

WHAT ARE GIT REPOSITORIES?

Repositories in Git refer to a collection of files that contain the different versions of the same project. These files are imported from the repository to the node, i.e. the local system of the developers for further changes and developments to the contents of the file. The version control system (VCS) software creates these versions and subsequently stores them in the Repositories. Using the various Git tools at our disposal in order to furnish copies of the existing Git repository is referred to as the process of cloning. Once we are done with the process of cloning, a copy of the repository is received by the user to work on.

Users are allowed to create a new repository as well as delete an existing one. The most convenient way of deleting a repository is by deleting the folder that contains it. Based on their usage in the server, repositories can be divided into two kinds: Bare Repositories and Non-Bare Repositories. The former is exclusively meant for sharing, while the latter can be edited and modified as per the needs and aims of the developer. Unless a parameter has been specified through code during the cloning process, it, by default, creates Non-Bare repos that act as working copies for developers.

- **Working area:** A working tree refers to a set of files that have originated from a particular version of a repository. A working tree will be able to keep track of the changes made by a particular user in a version of the repository. Whenever an operation is to be conducted, Git will only look through the files in the working area, and not all of the modified files. Even for commit operations, only the files present in the working area are considered by Git. The working tree user gets to change files by creating new files, as well as by modifying or removing the existing files. There are a few stages a file goes through in the working tree of a Git repository:

- **Modified:** When changes have been made to a file, but those changes are yet to be staged.

- **Staged:** The file has been committed and lies in the working area, for the next commit to take place.

- **Tracked:** When the Git repository is able to track a file, i.e. the file has been committed but not staged in the working directory.

- **Untracked:** Git repository is unable to track a file, implying that the file has neither been staged nor committed.

After making changes in the working area, the user can update these modifications to the Git repository, or even revert them. A Git repository is a safe space to perform a number of operations that will eventually create different versions of a particular project file. These operations might include creating a new repository or deleting an old one, the addition of files, committing an action, etc. After performing the required modifications in the working area, you have to save these changes to the local repository. To do this, first add your changes to the Index, i.e. the staging area, followed by committing those indexed changes to your local repository. You can add your changes to the index by making use of the git add command. The committing process, on the other hand, is done through the use of the git commit command. In addition to this, Git makes use of the push and pull commands in order to allow the user to synchronize their local repositories with repositories on remote servers, i.e. the nodes of other developers.

RECORDING CHANGES TO REPOS

After you have a Git repository on your system as well as the working copies of all its files, you now need to start making changes based on your development needs as well as committing snapshots of the same changes into your repository every time your project reaches a state of existence that you feel you need to record. Needless to say, saving or recording changes in a Git repository as well as for other VCSs is a more nuanced process than saving in traditional file editing applications, word processors, etc. The Git equivalent of saving is "committing". While the traditional understanding of saving implies a file system operation that either overwrites an existing file or writes a new one, the Git commit is an operation acting on a compendium of directories and files, as the abbreviation VCS (which Git is an example of) should at least partially clarify.

Saving changes in Git is also different from saving changes in a different kind of a VCS, say Subversion (SVN). SVN's commits, also known as "check-ins" make remote pushes to a centralized server. So SVN, unlike Git, needs proper access to the Internet, to record changes made to its projects. The Git commits, on the other hand, can be built up and easily captured via the local node only, and later pushed to a remote server, as and when needed, by making use of the git push-u origin main command. The difference between the way these two systems record changes can be attributed to their different structural designs. While Git is a distributed application model, SVN is a centralized VCS. Distributed applications are generally considered to be more robust since they are not hyper-dependent on a centralized server.

When you edit files, Git records them as modified since you have changed them after your last commit. As your work progresses, you will stage some of the modified files and then commit the changes made, and the cycle will go on in this manner.

The git status command is the command you need to look for to determine which state a particular file is in .git add is what you will have to use so that your system can begin tracking a new file. So, if you wish to track the xyz file, you need to do the following:

```
$ git add xyz
```

This file will now be tracked by the system, and shall be in the staging area for you to clean your commit. An important point to note about the git add command is that it takes the path name for either a file or directory; if it happens to be a directory, the command shall add all the files in your directory recursively. git add is a multi-purpose command, you use it to track new files as well as stage files, apart from marking conflict-riddled merge files as resolved. Furthermore, Git stages a particular file exactly as it was when you decided to use the git add command. If and when you choose to commit, the version of the chosen file as it was when you had last run the git add command will be how it shall be going in the commit, not the version of the file as it had looked in your working directory when you were running the git commit. So if you happen to modify a file after running the git add command, you need to run it again to stage the latest version of your file.

The results provided by the git status command are pretty impressive. However, they are also quite verbose. Git also happens to have a short status flag that allows you to see your changes in a more concise fashion. Untracked files are usually marked with the sign "??", "A" is used to indicate new files that have been recently added to the staging area, modified files are marked with an "M", etc. Additionally, the output will have two columns, the left-hand column is used to indicate the status of the staging area, while the right-hand column will tell you the present status of the working tree. If a file was modified, staged, then modified again, it will contain changes that are both staged and unstaged.

There will always be a few kinds of files that you do not wish for your Git system to add or even show as being untracked. These mostly tend to be the automatically generated files like the log files as well as the files produced by your in-built systems. For them, use the command .gitignore. This will make sure that you avoid committing the files you actually do not want in your Git repository, like coding files (ending with ".o" or an ".a"), files names ending with a tilde (~), generated by text editors to mark temporary files, etc.

A few pointers to keep in mind vis-à-vis the norms for patterns for the file types to use for .gitignore are:

- Lines starting with # as well as the blank lines need to be ignored.

- You need to make sure that you apply standard glob patterns recursively throughout your entire working tree.

- You should start patterns with a forward slash (/) in order to avoid recursivity.

- To specify a directory, end your patterns with a forward slash, the sign '/'.

- For negating a particular pattern, use an exclamation mark (!).

Glob patterns are usually really simple and regular expressions that shells tend to use. You should use two asterisks for your code to match the nested directories, for example, a/**/z will match with a/z, a/b/z, a/b/c/z, a/b/c/d/z, a/b/c/d/e/z, and so on. Additionally, an asterisk (*) should match zero or more characters, [abc] will match any character that is inside the brackets, brackets containing characters separated using a hyphen [0-9] will match any of the characters between them, a question mark (?) should be able to match a single character, etc. In case you want to begin with a solid foundation for your project, you should make use of GitHub to give you a decently comprehensive list of .gitignore file examples that should be a part of your code. Moreover, it is possible for a repository to have one. gitignore file in the whole directory that gets recursively applied to the entire repository. But there are bound to be more .gitignore files in the sub-directories. In the case of the nested .gitignore files, the rules apply only for the files of that particular directory. The Linux Kernel, for example, contains 206 .gitignore files in its source repository.

While the git status command is useful for its own purposes, it will not tell you what exactly is the nature of the changes that have been made, just the files that have undergone a change. To know about the kind of change that has taken place, use the git diff command. It will tell you what all you have changed that is yet to be staged, and what has been staged but not yet committed (git diff—staged). git diff will tell you not just about the changed files, but also the patch that was reworked by you, like the lines that were added or removed, etc. However, git diff will tell you about all the changes since the last commit that are yet to be staged. If you have staged all your changes, git diff will give no output. Further, if you want a graphical or external diff viewing program for your project, run git difftool rather than git diff, as it lets you view your diffs in different softwares like vimdiff, emerge, etc.

Once the staging area is set up the way you want it to be, it is time to commit your changes. Anything unstaged, i.e. anything git add command hasn't been run on since you edited it, will not be a part of your commit. It will, however, remain as a modified file on your local disk. To put it simply, if you saw that everything had been staged when you last used git status, it is time for committing the changes. Committing initiates the editor of your choice, via the command line git commit. Your choice of the editor can be reconfigured through the Git settings that we had delved into in the earlier sections of this book.

Once you have created your first commit, you should also be able to see some output that the commit gives regarding itself, what the SHA-1 checksum of the commit is, how many files underwent a change, the lines that were added or removed from the commit, etc. A commit will also record a snapshot of the setup of your staging area. Anything that you did not stage lies modified, and you will have to make another commit, so as to make that change a part of your history. Every commit is necessarily accompanied by a snapshot of that particular stage, which can be recreated/revisited by the user later. Moreover, if the staging area is proving to be too complex for your workflow in the project, it can be skipped through a simple shortcut. Add the "-a" option to your git commit command, and Git should automatically be able to stage every file that was being tracked before the commit, thereby allowing you to skip the git add part. While this is a very convenient option, bear in mind that sometimes, it might cause you to include unnecessary and unwanted changes.

In order to remove a file from Git, make sure that you remove it from your tracked files, i.e. your staging area, and then commit. The git rm command should be able to do that, removing the file from your working directory lest it shows up as untracked the next time around. On the other hand, if you simply remove that file from your working directory, it will show up as unstaged in your git status output, i.e. a change that is yet to be staged for a commit. Further, if you had modified a particular file or sent it to the staging area, you can remove it using the -f option. This option acts as a safety feature, preventing the accidental elimination of data that is yet to be recorded using a snapshot or that otherwise cannot be recovered.

You might also want to try keeping the file in your working tree, while removing it from your staging area. So, store the file at a place where Git cannot track it anymore. This can be remarkably useful if you did not add something with the .gitignore file, and subsequently staged it, say a set of .a compiled files, or a huge log file, etc. and can be conducted using the—cached option. You should also be able to pass directories, file-glob patterns, files, etc. through the git rm command.

Unlike other VCSs, Git does not track file movement. When you rename a file in Git, it shall not store metadata to let you know that you renamed that file, though the system itself is smart about realizing that later on, after the action has been conducted.

Lastly, a couple of tips and tricks to help you conduct your work smoothly while recording changes to your repositories:

There are different sets of changes you will have to make as part of your development work. So, you should separate your bug fixes, improvements, new features, etc. into different, well-annotated commits for your team members to understand the purpose and the reasoning behind your work when it is being reviewed. This work will also prove significant while conducting merges.

To make your commits easily comprehensible for other team members, use the following structure:

Line 1: Details of the Changes made

Line 2: *Blank*

Line 3: Reason for the said changes

WORKING WITH REMOTES

In Git, a remote is a common repository that all the members of a team make use of in order to be able to exchange the changes they have made to the program. In many cases, the remote repository is stored on code hosting services like GitHub or an internal server. Unlike the local repository, a remote does not come along with a file tree of the project's present state. It merely contains the .git versioning data.

SVN makes use of one centralized repository that serves the developers as a communication hub, wherein collaboration takes place via the movement of changesets between the central repository and the working copies. Git, on the contrary, makes use of the distributed collaboration system, wherein every developer has a copy of their repository, containing its own branch structure and location history. Users cannot share a single changeset, but have to create a series of commits. Then, the software lets you share whole branches between repositories. These branches have to be subsequently merged. The git remote command then is a piece of the broader system at hand that is responsible for synchronizing the changes being made. The records registered through the utilization of the git remote command have to be used alongside git push, git pull, as well as the git fetch commands. All these commands play their own respective roles to facilitate the syncing responsibilities of the software.

Being able to manage your remote repositories is a very crucial aspect of successfully running a project on Git. The remote repositories contain different versions of the file you are supposed to be working on, that are being hosted on the Internet or a different server. There can be many of them, and for you, they will either be read-only files or the read/write kind of files. Collaboration with multiple developers will involve your abilities at managing these many remote repositories, as well as pushing and pulling the data to and from them, as and when you are required to share work. You must be able to remove repositories that are not relevant to your work, add other remote repositories, manage the remote branches, see if they are tracked or not, etc. We should be able to learn some remote management tips in this section:

- **Showing remotes:** The git remote command helps you see the remote servers that have been reconfigured by you. You should be able to see a list of the shortnames of remote handles that you specify. If you clone a repository, you should be able to see "origin", which is the default name of the server you cloned from in the Git system. Specifying "-v" should also show you the URLs stored by Git to ensure the use of shortnames while reading and writing to that remote repository. If you are working on a repository with several remotes, the commands will list them all. So pulling contributions from the other users should be fairly doable.

- **Adding remote repositories:** We know how the git clone command surreptitiously adds the origin remote for your use. However, you can also add a new remote explicitly. For this purpose, you need to use the git remote add <shortname> <url> command. Using string pb within the command can further replace the use of the entire URL.

Pulling and Fetching from remote repositories—To get data from your remote projects, run the command:

```
$ git fetch <remote>
```

This command should be able to go to that remote repository and pull down the data from that remote project that you need to have. This will give you references to all the branches from that repository, which you can choose to examine or merge anytime. On the cloning of a repository, the command tends to automatically add it under the name "origin". So, the command git fetch origin fetches any recent work that has been pushed to the server since you last cloned it/fetched from it. The git fetch command will only download the data to the local repository, it will not modify anything or even merge the fetched data to your work. You will have to do so manually whenever you are ready. If your branch is currently set to track a branch of a remote repository, the git pull command will do a good job of fetching as well as merging that remote branch with the branch you are presently working on. This should entail a comfortable workflow for you, since by default, the git clone command will set up the local master branch so that it can track the master branch of the remote repository on the server you used for the purposes of cloning. From Git Version 2.27, the git pull command will keep giving you warnings until you do not configure the pull.rebase variable.

Additionally, in order to set the default behavior of Git, use the command:

```
git config -- global pull.rebase "false"
```

To rebase while pulling: git config -- global pull. rebase "true"

- **Pushing to remotes:** If you have a project you want to share with others, you shall have to push it upstream. The required command is: git push <remote> <branch>. If you wish to push the "master" branch to the "origin" server (cloning should set up these names for you), use the following command to push your commits:

```
$ git push origin master
```

This will work only if you have cloned from a server to which you have access to write. Additionally, nobody else must have pushed in the meanwhile. If you and another developer are cloning at the same time, and s/he pushes upstream, followed by you pushing upstream, your push, i.e. the latter push will be rejected, and rightly so. You then will have to fetch the work they have done and incorporate it into yours, before you are allowed to push again.

Ultimately, it should be easy to synchronize between multiple git repositories, particularly pushing to multiple remotes. Make sure that you are able to maintain multiple mirrors, i.e. copies of the same repository. Then, all you have to do is set up several push URLs on a remote, followed by using the git push command on that remote in a regular fashion.

- **Inspecting remotes:** To acquire more information about a particular remote, use the git remote show <remote> command. This should give you the remote repository's URL, alongside the tracking branch information. This command lists the remote references it has pulled down. It also usefully informs you that if you run the git pull command while being on the master branch, it will be automatically merging the remote's master branch with the local one after it is fetched. Another important command providing you with extensive information is the git remote show. It will tell you which branch has been automatically pushed to when you run the git push command on some branches. Further, it will inform you about the remote branches on the servers that you do not yet have access to, the remote branches that were removed, as well as the local branches which should be able to merge automatically with the remote branches if you were to run the git pull command.

- **Removing and renaming remotes:** With the command git remote rename, you will be able to change a remote's shortnames. A shortname is actually a key to your remote location. So, if it happens that you have more than one remote location in your local repository, you will not have to type out URLs repeatedly. Notably, changing a remote's shortname will lead to changes in the remote-tracking branch names too. If you change xyz to abc, what had been referenced as xyz/master will now be available at abc/master.

Additionally, if you want to remove a remote, say, because a contributor has left, or a server has been moved, make use of the command git remote remove or alternatively, git remote rm. If you delete the reference to a remote in this manner, all the associated configuration settings, as well as remote-tracking branches shall also be eliminated.

GIT ALIASES

One of the features that will undoubtedly make your Git experience easier: aliases. If you plan to work on Git consistently, aliases are something that you ought to familiarize yourself with. If you have only typed out your text partially, there is no way for Git to automatically comprehend your command. If you do not wish to type the whole text while using the many commands that you will have to on Git, you can always use the git config command so that you can set up an alias for those commands that you tend to use frequently.

Although the Graphical User Interface (GUI) of Git is very useful when it comes to ensuring an integrated development environment (IDE), like Visual Studio (VS) Code, Intelli, etc. at other times, you will have to resort to command-line interface (CLI) for better work and higher productivity. A CLI is usually defined as a user interface of an application, which accepts a line at a time typed in commands. The program that handles such an interface is known as a command-line processor or a command-line interpreter. Today, most users tend to rely on GUIs as well as menu-driven interactions. But, some maintenance and programming jobs might not have a GUI at all, preferring instead to use command lines only. The CLI programs are better handled via scripting. Many software systems make use of CLIs for the purposes of control and operation. This also includes utility programs as well as programming environments, in general.

The term "alias" is synonymous with the word "short-cut". Alias creation is also available in utilities like bash shell, a command language as well as a Unix shell developed by GNU Project's Brian Fox as a software replacement for the Bourne shell. Aliases create shorter commands which map for the long commands. They ensure more efficient workflows since lesser keystrokes are needed to execute a particular command. For example, via the use of the command: "$git config --global alias.ci commit", you will now have to use git ci whenever you want to refer to git commit in your code. Similarly, the git checkout command is also a frequently used command in Git, adding up a significant number of cumulative keystrokes over a period of time. Here, you can always create an alias mapping git co with git checkout, which should save precious fingertip power as well as effort through a shorter keystroke form, by the typing of "git co". As you move on your development journey with Git, you will have to use a plethora of commands; so it will not hurt to make convenient aliases for each one of them. Not only that, you are also allowed to create commands that you think should exist. For example, if you face usability issues while unstaging a file, you should add your own unstage alias to Git. Basically, Git will replace every command with the alias you have created for it. However, there will be instances where you want to run an external command, and not the Git subcommand. For cases like that, you should begin your command with the "!" character. This will be particularly useful for the developers who write their own tools to work with a proper Git repository.

For the git search commit, Git alias allows you to define many complex aliases, like executing the external shell commands, executing custom scripts as well as more layered commands, like those for shell pipes, etc. For example, you could define these alias to conduct searches within your commits, as well as to search for particular strings, as per your wants and needs.

It is crucial to remember that there is no specific command for git aliases. Aliases are to be created via the use of the git config command as well as Git's configuration files. The git config command is a very useful command that helps in the quick creation of aliases. It is a helper command so that we can write to the local as well as the global Git config files. Here, the values in a local file shall apply only to a single repository, while the configuration values of a global file apply to a single user. Git utilizes a hierarchical approach toward configuration, wherein the settings of a broader scope are to be inherited, if not straight-up overridden. At the top level is the system config, for all users, that is stored in/etc/git. This is followed by the global config that can override the system defaults with the personal ones, and is located inside the home directory of the user, for example, $HOME/.config/git/config or $HOME/.gitconfig. Lastly, there is the local config for a particular repository, located at .git/config in the repository root, i.e. the repo's .git directory, which should be able to override the other aforementioned configs, to be able to set specific options for the repositories. The local configuration applies to the context repository that git config gets invoked in. If you do not specify which level you want to work with, the local config will be chosen by the software as default. Basically, all the different kinds of configuration files share the same syntax, but have different scopes, offering the user a lot of flexibility while working on the development of a particular project. Like for other configuration files, the scope of aliases can be local as well as global. These local and global config files can be manually edited as well as saved, in order to create aliases. The global config file is stored at the file path $HOME/.gitconfig. On the other hand, the local path is found within the active git repository/.git/config. Another example of how an alias section should look like:

```
[alias]
co = checkout
Co here is a shortcut for the word
"checkout".
```

Also, creating aliases implies creating only shortcuts. The source commands are not modified, compromised, or devalued in any fashion. The git checkout command is still open and available for use, though now, we have the option of using the git co alias as well, which serves our purposes better. The aliases are also created using the—global flag, which means that they are to be stored in the Git's global operating system level configuration file. On the Linux systems, for example, the global config file is found in the User's home directory at /.gitconfig.

Git, thus, offers its users the ability to make aliases the equivalents of the source commands. For utilizing aliases to create new Git commands, remove the recently added files from the staging area. This can be done through leveraging options to the command git reset. A new alias will have to be created in order to encapsulate this behavior, along with a new alias-command-keyword, which should ideally be easy to remember. Aliases wrap the standard git commands into a new, faux, but convenient command. You should be able to see the entire set of aliases by listing your configuration using the Git command git config. Even though aliases can be defined by using shells like Bash or Zsh, utilizing Git over them will offer you a set of advantages. Firstly, you will be able to use your aliases across a number of shells without needing any kind of additional configuration. If Git is defining your aliases for you, you will also be able to take advantage of native integration with Git's autocorrect feature, wherein Git will suggest aliases as alternatives if you happen to accidentally mistype a command. Lastly, Git will save your aliases in the user's configuration file, so that you should be able to transfer them to other machines by simply copying a single file. Irrespective of the methods you use, defining aliases will definitely improve your overall experience of conducting project development work through Git. Some of the useful aliases you can make on Git are following:

- **Git status:** Git command-line users have to make use of the status command to be able to see changed or untracked files. This command, by default, gives out verbose output with a lot of lines, that the user does not necessarily want or require. Here, you should make use of a single alias in order to address both of the components: ensure the definition of alias as st in order to shorten the command to be used with the option of "-sb". This should output a less lengthy status along with the provided branch information. If you make use of this alias on a perfectly clean branch, your output should look something like this:

```
$ git st
## master
```

Making use of it on a branch that has untracked as well as changed files should produce the result:

```
$ git st
## master
 M test2
?? test3
```

- **Git last commit:** This command is used to give you details about the very last commit you made.

- **Git log --one line:** You can create this alias to make sure that your commits are displayed purely as single lines in order to lead to a more concise output.

```
$ git config --global alias.ll 'log
--oneline'
```

- **Git commit:** The command git commit is to be used when you are making a lot of changes to a particular Git repository. The git commit -m command can be made much more efficient with the use of the cm alias.

- **Git Remote:** The command git remote -v lists out all the remote repositories that have been configured. This command can be shortened by making use of the alias rv.

```
$ git config --global alias.rv 'remote
-v'
```

- **Git Diff:** This command displays the differences between the files in various different commits, as well as the differences between a commit and the working tree. It can be shortened and simplified by making use of the d alias. The standard git diff command should work perfectly fine when you have to make small changes. But in case the changes required are complex and multi-layered, you are advised to make use of an external tool like vimdiff to make things easier for yourself. The alias dv should be able to display diffs using vimdiff. So, you need to create it, and subsequently use the parameter -y in order to be able to skip the confirmation prompt.

- **Git Config List:** Using the gl alias should make it easier for you to list all the user configurations available. This should also allow you to see all the defined aliases, alongside other configuration options.

Ultimately, Git aliases are an immensely useful feature that can tremendously improve your efficiency through the optimization of the execution of several repetitive and common commands. Git has not put a limit on the number of aliases to be used, so you should be able to define as many of them as you need to, and many developers do.

Conversely, you can choose to use aliases only for your most-used commands, since defining many of them shall make it harder for you to memorize them, and you will have to look them up in order to be able to use them, neutralizing the ergonomic benefits they are supposed to provide to you as well as to your organization.

For better Git aliases, you can also mine your CLI history. CLI improvements usually have the potential to tremendously improve your workflow. Aliases are useful, but which aliases are the most suitable for you? We have provided a list of common commands whose aliases you can make above. But you would have to know what your most-used commands are, right? You should probably be able to guess the most used command in your work, or perhaps even the top two, but there are many you will simply be clueless about. This is where you can let your CLI history intervene on your behalf. Our focus here is on git aliases, but this strategy should work very well for command-line tools you make use of, as well.

The first step is to use the command history to find out what commands you run most frequently. The command history should be able to print every line that you have run recently in your shell, that too in a chronological order. This is going to give us the data that we need, making use of history, the filters used for various git commands, counting of the repeated lines, as well as sorting them by the repeated count. Use head -n X if you just want the search to focus on top x results. The results from this code should give you significant information about your most-used commands, allowing you to begin creating your aliases. However, you must keep some catches in mind. For example, if the git commit command doesn't come up in your results at all, this is probably because the commits might contain inline messages, and therefore each commit is treated as unique by the software.

Using this wisdom, you should be able to reframe your commands, to get better, more specific results, that serve and satisfy the concerns of your work in a meaningful fashion.

TAGGING

Let's begin by defining tagging, and how it involves the use of the git tag command. Tags are references that point to some specific points that are contained in the git history. Tagging is utilized to capture a particular point in history, and made use of for a marked version release. A tag, then, is a branch that is immune to any kind of change. Tags, unlike branches, will not have a history of commits after being created. The Git software allows you to create tags, delete them, list them all, share them, etc.

Like the other VCSs, Git can tag specific points in a repository's history as being significant. People usually make use of this functionality provided by the software to mark out the release points (v1.0, v2.0, etc.). By the end of this section, you should be able to have an elementary understanding of how you can create as well as delete tags, how you can list existing tags, what those various kinds of tags are, etc.

How to List Your Tags?

In Git, listing the tags constitutes a fairly straightforward process. Type "git tag" (with either -l or -list):

```
$ git tag
v1.0
v2.0
```

You should get a list of all your tags arranged in an alphabetical order. The said order, in which they are placed, however, is not of any relevance to us. You can also conduct searches to look for tags that match a certain pattern. The Git source repo happens to contain more than five hundred tags. Do remember that choosing between the -l or -list option is mandatory if you want your software to list out tag wildcards. This is optional when you just want the whole list of tags, because here, the command git tag, when you run it, shall be implicitly assuming that you want a listing, and so it will provide you one. But if you are supplying a wildcard pattern to the software, it expects you to choose between -l or -list to be able to match tag names.

Creating Tags

There are two kinds of tags that Git offers—lightweight and annotated. A lightweight tag is like a branch that doesn't change much; it is only a pointer to a particular command. The annotated tags, however, are stored in the Git database as complete objects. They contain a lot of extra metadata like the tagger name, email, as well as date, are checksummed, contain a tagging message, and are to be signed as well as verified using GNU Privacy Guard, abbreviated as GPG. Like commits as well as commit messages, the annotated tags are accompanied by a tagging message. It is further recommended that you should be able to create annotated tags in order to acquire all this information; nevertheless, lightweight tags are also available to be worked with in case you only want a temporary tag, and do not want to retain other information.

Annotated Tags

The process of creating an annotated tag in Git is fairly simple. You just have to specify "-a" when you have to run the tag command. "-m" stands for tagging message, which is to be stored with the tag. Git also tends to launch your editor if you fail to specify a message to go along with your annotated tag, so that you are able to type it in. By using the git show command, you should also be able to see the tag data alongside the commit which has been tagged. This should also show you the date the commit was tagged on, the tagger information, as well as the annotation message available.

Lightweight Tags

Commits can also be tagged by utilizing lightweight tags. This includes the commit checksum which is stored in a file, and where no other information is to be kept. In order to create a lightweight tag, you just need to provide a tag name, rather than supplying options like -a, -s, -m, etc. For lightweight tags, the git show command will just show you the commit, and not the extra tag information that comes with it, which was visible in the case of annotated tags.

Tagging Later

You can tag commits even after you have moved away from them. Let's say you forgot to tag a project, of a specific commit. You need not worry because this issue can be resolved after the fact. To tag your commit now, make sure that you specify the commit checksum, or at least a part of it, at the end of your command. Post this, you should be able to see that your commit has now been tagged.

You should also be well-versed with how you can tag your old commits. By default, the git tag should be able to create a tag on your commit that the Head is referring to. Alternatively, the git tag can be passed around as a reference point for a specific commit. This should be able to tag your passed commit instead of defaulting it to Head. If you need to gather the list of all your older commits, you can do so via the execution of the git log command.

Sharing Tags

The git push command cannot transfer tags to remote servers on its own. You shall have to explicitly push your tags to a shared server after you create them. This process is akin to sharing remote branches; you should be able to carry it out by running the command git push origin <tagname>. If you have many tags, and you wish to push them all at once, you are recommended to use the—tags option for the git push command. This will ensure the transfer of all your tags to the remote server, that aren't already there. So, now if someone will pull from your repository, or simply clone it, they should be able to acquire all of your tags simultaneously. However, do keep in mind that the git push command will push both annotated as well as lightweight tags. This is because currently, the Git software does not offer us any option of being able to push only the lightweight tags. However, if you intend to push only the annotated tags to your remote repositories, you should use the git push <remote> -follow-tags.

Deleting Tags

In order to delete a tag from your local repository, you would have to use the command git tag -d <tagname>.

However, remember that the tags will not be removed from the remote servers. In order to be able to do so, there are two command variations you will need to learn to use. The first kind is git push <remote> :refs/tags/<tagname>. The code used here can be basically interpreted as a null tag value that is being pushed to the remote tag, in effect deleting it. The second type of command for the purpose of deleting a tag is more intuitive:

```
$ git push origin --delete <tagname>
```

Check Out the Tags

To see the versions of the different files that a tag is pointing to, you will have to utilize the command git checkout with respect to that particular tag, even though this will put your repository in a "detached head" state, which can lead to significant side-effects. In the "detached head" state, if you make modifications and then create a commit, the tag will be able to stay the same, but the new commit shall not belong to any branch and will be pretty much, inaccessible, except if you make use of its exact commit hash address location. So, if you have to make changes, like fixing the bug of an older version of a particular software, you will have to create another branch. If you do this as well as make the commit, the branch created will be slightly different than the tag since it will be moving forward with new changes, so you have to be careful while dealing with this aspect of checking out your tags.

Apart from this, Git also allows you to tag the contents of a single file without requiring its file name in any manner whatsoever. Having said that, these tags tend to have limited utility. Tags are expected to point us in the direction of commits, and the special tags intended for the non-commits tend to display variations in their behavior; for example, you will not be able to check out these special tags. So, it is strongly recommended that you never make use of non-commit tags. When you want only some files of yours to be tagged, it is always better to use a separate repo for them, or different branches, given that git always tends to go through the whole tree in order to check its operations.

You can tag a commit only as a snapshot in order to record the history of your repository. Git stores these files as blobs, and you should make use of git notes to add any form of supplementary information to these blobs. However, keep in mind that the note is attached to a particular blob, so if the file changes a blob, and acquires a new one, implying a new SHA-1 hash value, the new blob will not retain the same note.

Retagging or Replacing Old Tags

If you attempt creating a new tag with the same identifier as that of an already existing tag, Git will show an error message. Furthermore, if you make an attempt to tag an older commit with a preexisting tag identifier, Git will again display the same error. In that event, you will have to update an existing tag, i.e. the -f FORCE option will have to be used.

With this, our discussion of Tagging comes to an end. In this chapter, we attempted to focus on several aspects of what working with Git Repositories entails, the definition of repositories, how we can record changes to our repos, working with Remotes, git aliases, as well as tagging. The next chapter will be able to provide you with a detailed discussion on working with branches, the definition of branches, branching and merging, branch workflows as well as remote branches. Read on.

CHAPTER 4

Working with Branches

IN THIS CHAPTER

> ➤ What are branches?

> ➤ Branching and Merging

> ➤ Branch Workflows

> ➤ Remote Branches

In the previous chapter, we learnt about Git Repositories through our extensive discussions on recording change to repos, working with Remotes, Git aliases, tagging, etc. In this chapter, we will shift the focus of our discussion to branches, as we will read and learn about Git branches, branching and merging, branch workflows as well as remote branches. So, let's begin with alacrity.

DOI: 10.1201/9781003229100-4

WHAT ARE BRANCHES?

In this section, we will be conducting a detailed exposition of the Git branch command, as well as a discussion of the Git branching model, in general. Code branching allows the software development teams to be able to work on the different aspects of a particular project without impacting each other's efforts. This system ensures efficient organization in a shared codebase, conducted via the processes like merging as well as branching.

A branch is supposed to be a copy of a codeline, which is to be managed by the version control system (VCS). Branches allow for parallel work, along with a well-demarcated separation of work-in-progress code with the stable as well as tried-and-tested code. The codebase of a VCS is variously referred to as a baseline, master, mainline, or trunk. The software, Perforce, for example, makes use of the term mainline. Developers have to work individually, so therefore, they create branches, with direct or indirect origin from the mainline, in order to be able to experiment in isolation. This ensures the stability of the overall project/product. It is a very good practice to keep on updating the working branches with changes made in the code. This is done in VCSs through the process of merging.

Branching inevitably leads to the establishment of a relationship between the branch as well as the main codeline that the branch diverged from. As one developer keeps on working on their own branch, others might also be submitting their changes to the central codeline. So, merging needs to be a consistent and frequently-done practice, particularly to ensure minimal conflicts with the work of other developers. A lot of VCSs, like TFS, SVN, Git, etc.

avoid a systematic tracking of the relationships between branches. In case a developer wants to submit her/his changes, they need to figure out where they need to conduct the merge. In order to properly grapple with this issue, the companies devote a lot of their resources in order to implement complex (and costly) scripting for their respective VCSs. Furthermore, they might also outline an established branching strategy, that everyone is largely expected to adhere to. The fact is that as projects, teams, as well as codebases continue to grow, the potential issues around the processes of branching will also become more complex and tough to handle. As it is, with thousands or even hundreds of developers working on the code of the same project almost simultaneously, it becomes next to impossible to be able to keep track of everything.

The feature of branching is available in several VCSs available in the market, at present. In VCSs other than Git, branching is often an expensive process with regard to your time as well as the disk space available. In Git, however, the branches are a daily part of the developmental process. Git branches basically point to a snapshot of the changes you have made to your code. If you wish to include a new feature or fix an irritant bug, no matter how big or small the development is supposed to be, you will inevitably end up spawning a new branch in order to be able to encapsulate those changes. Branching, thus, makes it harder to allow bad and unstable code to be able to get merged in the central code base, giving you a chance to clean up your history before carrying out a merge into the main branch. Via branching, a repository can sustain multiple parallel lines of isolated development by each of its developers, for different features of the project at hand. Apart from this, branching also contributes to keeping the main branch impervious to questionable code. As mentioned previously, the implementation of Git branches is much more convenient than the models of other VCSs. Rather than copying files from directory to directory, Git is able to store a branch as a reference to a specific commit. So, the branch itself is not a container of commits, but every branch is representative of the tip of a sequence of commits. The history of any branch can be extrapolated via the relationships of commits to one another.

Here, it is also important to realize that Git branches are unlike the branches of Subversion (SVN). While SVN branches are only able to capture the large-scale development effort, that too rarely, Git branches tend to play an integral role to carry out your everyday workflow. Now, let's delve into Git's internal branching architecture in a more detailed fashion.

Working

A branch is supposed to represent an independent line of development. Branches are an abstract form of the editing-staging-committing process. Branches give you a completely fresh staging area, project history, as well as working directory. Any new commit created is to be recorded in the history of the current branch, resulting in a fork in the working history of the project. The git branch commands allow you to create, rename, list, as well as delete the branches. However, the commands available on the software cannot allow you to switch between multiple branches, or combine a forked history that had been divided earlier. This is the reason why the git branch is so perfectly integrated with the git merge as well as the git checkout commands.

Common Commands

- **git branch:** It provides a list of all the branches in your repository. Another synonymous command for it is the git branch—list.

- **git branch <branch>:** Should be able to create a new branch called "branch". This will not allow you to be able to check out the new branch.

- **git branch -d <branch>:** Will delete the specified branch for you. This is a "safe" command because Git will not delete the branch if it happens to contain unmerged changes.

- **git branch -D <branch>:** A modification of the previous command that will force delete the mentioned branch, despite it having unmerged changes. You can use this command if you wish to permanently do away with all the commits affiliated with a specific type of development.

- **git branch -m <branch>:** Will rename the current branch to <branch>.

- **git branch -a:** Will list out all the remote branches of the project file.

Creation of Branches

It is desirable and imperative for us to restate that branches are just supposed to be pointers for the commits. Whenever you will create a new Git branch, Git will simply just add a new pointer. There is no need to change the history of the repository in any manner whatsoever. After creating a branch, you are expected to follow it up with the creation of commits, using the commands git checkout, the standard git add, as well as the git commit commands.

Creation of Remote Branches

All of the aforementioned examples have demonstrated local branch operations. The git branch command too tends to work on remote branches only. In order to be able to operate on remote branches, you will first have to configure a remote repo, and subsequently add it to the local repo config. This command should be able to push a copy of the local branch toward the remote repo.

Deleting Branches

Once you have completed your work on a branch, and have merged it to the main codebase as well, you will be well-advised to delete the branch without having to lose any history. However, you will end up receiving an error message if you attempt to delete a branch without having merged it. This should protect you from losing access to a whole line of development that you might have worked very hard on. If you must delete the branch anyhow, you could, as mentioned previously as well, use the command git branch -D <branch>, which will force delete the branch whether it has been merged or not. Because it will eliminate a branch irrespective of its status, and without giving you a second warning, make sure you are careful with it and use it with good jurisprudence. The previously mentioned commands will be able to eliminate only a local copy of the branch. It is very much possible that the branch still exists on a remote repo. In order to eliminate a remote branch, you will have to use the following command: git push origin --delete "file name".

BRANCHING AND MERGING

As we learnt in the previous section, you can make use of Git in order to create branches for your project/s. Git branching makes sure that multiple developers are able to work on a particular project by being able to modify the working codebase.

In this section, you shall be able to learn more about Git branching, the various ways of creating branches, as well as how we should be able to merge the said branches to a remote or local repository.

Definition of Git Branching

Git branching is a tremendously useful feature because it permits the developers to fork out of the production version of code in order to be able to add a feature, or fix a bug, etc. Developers create branches to be allowed to work with a copy of the central code without having to modify the existing version. The creation of branches allows you to isolate the changes you want to make to the copy of your code, which you will be well-advised to test before merging it into the main branch.

Ensure remembering that there is nothing exceptional or special in the main branch. It is simply the first copy that was put to use to initialize the Git repository through the use of the git init command. When you create a commit, Git's software is able to identify the snapshot of files taken up using a unique SHA-1 hash address. SHA-1 (Secure

Hash Algorithm 1) is a kind of cryptographic hash function which takes in an input and follows up by producing a 160-bit (or 20 byte) hash value that is known as a message digest. This message is usually rendered as a hexadecimal number, which is 40 digits long. Revision Control Systems like Git, Monotone, Mercurial, etc. make use of SHA-1, not for security crucially, but in order to be able to identify multiple revisions, as well as ensure that the data has not changed in any way, due to accidentally caused corruption. Linus Torvalds, the creator of Git, has said this about SHA-1,[1]

> If you have disk corruption, if you have DRAM corruption, if you have any kind of problems at all, Git will notice them. It's not a question of *if*, it's a guarantee. You can have people who try to be malicious. They won't succeed. ... Nobody has been able to break SHA-1, but the point is the SHA-1, as far as Git is concerned, isn't even a security feature. It's purely a consistency check. The security parts are elsewhere, so a lot of people assume that since Git uses SHA-1 and SHA-1 is used for cryptographically secure stuff, they think that, Okay, it's a huge security feature. It has nothing at all to do with security, it's just the best hash you can get. ...
>
> I guarantee you, if you put your data in Git, you can trust the fact that five years later, after it was converted from your hard disk to DVD to whatever new technology and you copied it along, five years later you can verify that the data you get back out is the exact same data you put in. ...

[1] https://www.youtube.com/watch?v=4XpnKHJAok8&t=3380s and https://en.wikipedia.org/wiki/SHA-1#Data_integrity, last edited Jan. 14, 2022

One of the reasons I care is for the kernel, we had a break in on one of the BitKeeper sites where people tried to corrupt the kernel source code repositories. However Git does not require the second preimage resistance of SHA-1 as a security feature, since it will always prefer to keep the earliest version of an object in case of collision, preventing an attacker from surreptitiously overwriting files.

So, when you shall initially create a branch, Git basically creates a new pointer to the same commit that the main branch is presently working on. As you go along your coding journey and create new commits in your branch, Git will ensure the creation of new pointers to keep track of all the changes you have been making. The latest commits come ahead of the commits of the central branch. Subsequently, each branch will take track of its own file versions. Git comes to know which branch you have checked out by making use of a special pointer called HEAD. Whenever you create a new branch, Git does not immediately change the HEAD pointer to a new branch. Nevertheless, you should be able to see HEAD when you create new branches, and subsequently view their commit logs. This branching function makes Git really powerful. Several people create multiple branches so that they can work on their code, and later merge their changes to the main branch. Branches are supposed to be temporary, and need to be deleted when the work has been completed.

Branch Naming

You can name branches anything you like. However, your organization or the project you are currently working on, might have standardized rules for branch naming conventions. For example, you might be recommended to name a particular branch based on the first, last, full name, or initials, etc. of the person who was responsible for working on that branch as well as a concise description of the work item. You could also name a branch as per its function, whether it works on a feature, bug fix, hotfix, etc. Furthermore, you could name a branch after its different development cycles. As more projects and work items come up, you can create a branch for that item, from its particular branch. Not only that, you can create branches from other branches as well.

To create a branch, use the git branch command, and follow it up with the name of the branch. After creating the branch, you can use the git branch command again to be able to view all the available branches. Creating a branch will not automatically switch, and take you to the newly created branch. Git tends to use an asterisk, as well as a differently colored font to identify which branch is currently active.

If you have to create a new branch and checkout that branch simultaneously, make use of the git checkout command. After this command is completed, Git has moved its HEAD to a new branch.

Git also allows you to create a branch from a previous commit on a currently existing branch. A commit is simply a snapshot in time of a particular bunch of files in a Git repository. You will create a branch out of a commit if you wish to work on a particular snapshot of the files. Before the creation of the branch, you must know the SHA-1 identifier of the commit. You will have to make use of the git log command to view the previous commits as well as find the identifier that you are looking for. Each commit should have a complete SHA-1 hash as its identifier. Nevertheless, the first few characters should suffice for you to actually identify the commit.

If you work on the development of specific features or bug fixes, you are probably used to creating branches out of branches to work on an item. Creating a new branch out of an existing branch is no different than creating a branch out of the main branch. You will have to specify the name of the other branch in order to initiate the command.

You sometimes will also have to download a branch from a remote repository in order to be able to work. Just as you have a local copy of a repository to work with, so do your other colleagues. These developers have branches they are working on, and they can push these branches to a remote repository. Along your way, you might have to work on another branch that is not local to your system. You will have to pull or download those specific branches from a remote repository so that you are able to use it on your system. In order to retrieve a branch from a remote repository, use the git pull command against the origin as well as specify the name of the branch. If you now check through the list of all the available branches, the new branch shall not appear automatically. Nevertheless, you can checkout this branch, as well as begin working on it as well.

Once you are done with the developmental work on the new branch, you will have to combine it into the main branch. Merging will take up the changes you have made to your existing branch, and subsequently combine them with the main branch. There are two ways Git utilizes to perform the task of merging history, depending on the commit history involved, the fast forward, and the three-way merge. In the case of the former, when you have to combine a particular branch with the main branch, Git will compel the main branch pointer to move ahead to a commit with a shared ancestor. In the case of the three-way merge, Git tends to take snapshots of three different commits so that it is able to create a new one.

To merge branches locally, i.e. in a local repository, use the command git checkout, so that you are able to switch to the branch that you eventually want to merge into. This branch is usually the main branch. Next, you will have to make use of the command git merge so that you can specify the name of the branch that is to be merged, and subsequently conduct the operation. Do note that this kind of a merge will come under the category of a fast-forward merge.

Now, we come to the question of merging your branches to remote repositories. If you have created a new branch in your local repository, the remote repository is obviously not aware of its existence. Before pushing your branch code into the remote repository, you will have to set the remote repository as an upstream branch. This is done by using the git push command. This command will not only set your upstream branch, but simultaneously push your branch contents to the remote repository.

You must also be well-versed with how to merge a Main into a branch. During the developmental work, other developers will surely merge their own work to the main branch, thus updating it. This means that your branch now is out-of-date and missing the full contents of the main branch. To resolve this issue, you need to merge the main branch into your own branch. For this, check out your branch, and subsequently make use of the git merge command.

BRANCH WORKFLOWS

The core principle behind the feature branch workflow is that the code development for one particular feature should be conducted on a separate branch rather than the main branch. This structure allows for multiple developers to be able to work on feature, without having to disturb the well-established main code. This, additionally ensures that the main branch shall never contain broken or bad code, which is a great advantage for the environments built for the sake of carrying out continuous integration. The encapsulation of feature development also allows for the developers to leverage pull requests, and allows for the initiation of discussions and deliberations around particular branch developments. They also allow the developers the ability to sign off from a feature before it gets integrated with the rest of the project. Additionally, if you find yourself stuck while working on a particular feature, you have the facility of opening a pull request to ask your colleagues for feedback as well as suggestions. The pull requests basically make it remarkably easy for the team members to provide comments on each other's work, fostering a spirit of cooperation as well as collaboration.

The Git Feature Branch Workflow then is a composable workflow that can also be leveraged by the other high-level Git workflows. It is branching model-focused, making it an important inspiration for the creation as well as the management of the branches. Other workflows tend to be more repo-focused. The Git Feature Branch Workflow can usually be easily incorporated into other kinds of workflows. For example, the Gitflow, as well as the Git Forking Workflow, traditionally use Git Feature Branch Workflow for their branching models.

How It Works

The Git Feature Branch Workflow assumes the presence of a central repository, with "main" representing the official history of the project at hand. Instead of making their commits directly on the local main branch, the developers have to create a new branch every time they must begin work on a new feature. Feature branches must ideally be given descriptive names like "Bug-Fix-603". The chief idea is to render a clear and focused purpose to every branch. Git has not established any technical distinctions between the main branch and the feature branches, so the developers should be able to easily edit, stage, as well as commit changes to a feature branch.

Additionally, you can and should push your feature branches to the central repository. This will make it possible for you to be able to share a feature with your development team members without tampering with the official code in any manner whatsoever. Since the main happens to be the only "special" branch, storing multiple feature branches on your central repository should hopefully not pose any problems. It also happens to be an easy and convenient method of ensuring a backup for the local commits of all the developers working on the team. Let us now go through the lifecycle of a feature branch:

Beginning with the Main Branch

All the feature branches are created from the latest code of a project. This state of the code is maintained and updated on the main branch. You can switch the repo to the main branch, pull the latest commits from it, and subsequently reset the repo's local copy of the main branch so that you can match it to the latest version of the code.

Creating a New Branch

You are supposed to use a separate branch for every issue or feature that you must work on. After the creation of the branch, you must check it out locally, and any changes that you shall make will be found on that branch.

Subsequent Tasks

Update, add, commit, and follow it up with pushing the changes. On your branch, make the edits, stage, as well as commit those changes in the regular fashion, developing your feature with as many commits as you deem necessary. When done, push your commits, updating your feature branch to Bitbucket, which is a Git-based source code repository hosting service that was launched in 2008.

Push Feature Branch to Remote

It is always a good idea to push your feature branch up toward the central repository. This should be able to serve as a convenient backup, particularly while you are collaborating with fellow developers, as this would give them the access to be able to view the commits to the new branch. This command also pushes new features to the central repository (origin), and the -u flag adds them as a remote-tracking branch. After setting up your tracking branch, the git push command can be invoked in order to automatically push the new feature branches to the central repository. If you need to get feedback on a new feature branch, you must create a pull request, preferably in systems providing repository management solutions like Bitbucket Data Center, Bitbucket Cloud, etc. They should be able to help you add reviewers, and subsequently, you must make sure that everything is okay before conducting your merges.

Resolve Feedback

Teammates can comment, provide feedback, and eventually approve of the pushed commits. You must resolve the comments locally, commit, and then push the suggested changes to Bitbucket. Your updates should appear in the pull request.

Merge Your Pull Request

Before merging, resolve the merge conflicts, if any. Merge conflicts are bound to occur if others have made changes to the repo. When your pull request does not contain any conflicts and is approved, you are free to add your code to the main branch. Merge using the pull request in Bitbucket.

Pull Requests

Apart from separating the feature development, branches allow the developers to discuss changes through pull requests. Once you have completed your work on a feature, you do not have to immediately merge it into the main.

Instead, you need to push the feature branch into the central server, and file a pull request that asks to merge their additions into the main. This will give the other developers an opportunity to review your work before it becomes part of the primary codebase.

Code review is considered to be a significant advantage of pull requests, but its design is actually supposed to facilitate a general way to talk and discuss about the code at hand. So pull requests can be understood as discussions pertaining to a specific branch. So, they can also be utilized quite early in the development process. For example, if you need help in the development of a particular feature, all you need to do is file a pull request. The interested parties, including hopefully your seniors, more experienced programmers, etc. will be notified automatically, and they should be able to see your question right next to the associated commits. Once a pull request has been accepted, the act of publishing the feature is pretty much the same as it is in the Centralized Workflow. First, make sure that you synchronize the local main with the upstream main. Then, merge the feature branch into the main, and subsequently, push back the updated main to the central repository. Pull requests should also be facilitated by product repository management solutions like Bitbucket Server, or Bitbucket Cloud.

Now, to better understand the workflow, let's take an example. Three coders A, B, and C, are working on a project together. The project involves a code review of a new feature pull request. Before developing the feature, A needs a separate branch to work on. He can request for the new branch through either checking out a branch based on main, or using the -b flag to create the branch in case it doesn't already exist. Using this branch, A edits, stages, as well as commits changes in a regular fashion, building the feature with as many commits as he deems necessary. A adds some commits to his feature during the morning. Now, before leaving for Lunch, it will be a good idea for him to push up his feature branch to the central repository. This will not only serve as a good backup, but if A has to collaborate with other developers, they should now have access to his initial commits. The git push command will push the branch in question to the origin, i.e. the central repository, and the -u flag can be utilized to add it as a remote-tracking branch. After the setup of the tracking branch, A can git push without any parameters in order to push his feature.

After his lunch, A is able to complete his feature. He files a pull request to let the rest of his team know that he's done, before merging his branch into the main. But, he also will have to ensure that the central repository has his most recent commits. After using the git push command, he files the pull request in his Git Graphical User Interface (GUI), asking to merge his feature into the main, and his team members are notified of it automatically. A positive aspect of the pull requests is that they are able to show comments next to the relevant commits, making it easy to put on questions about the relevant changesets.

Now, B receives the pull request, and looks through the feature branch that A worked on. He decides that he feels it might be useful to make a few alterations before integrating it with the official project. A and B then interact with each other via the pull request.

Now, in order to make the necessary changes, A uses the very same process he did to create the first iteration of his feature. He edits, stages, commits, and pushes his updates to the central repository in the end. All of this activity will be visible through the pull request, and B can look into it, and still make comments along the way. If he wanted, B could have also pulled A's branch in his local repository, and worked on it himself. Any commits that B might have added, if such a scenario had occurred, would have also shown up in the pull request.

Once B is prepared to accept the pull request, either A or B will have to merge the feature into the stable product. This leads to a merge commit, a symbolic fusion of the feature with the remaining code base. However, if you are partial to linear history, Git can also allow you to rebase the feature onto the main branch, before being able to execute the merge, leading to a fast-forward merge.

Several GUIs should be able to automate the acceptance process for pull requests by running all of the relevant commands just through the click of an "Accept" button. If your software does not have that facility, it should at least have the ability to automatically close the pull request whenever the feature branch gets merged into the main one.

C, in the meantime, has been doing the same thing. While A and B have been jointly working on A's feature, C has been on his own feature branch. By isolating different features into separate branches, everybody should be able to work independently, and yet, it is no big deal to be able to share your changes with fellow developers, and conduct deliberations, if you deem it necessary.

All in all, the Git Feature Branch Workflow helps you organize as well as track branches focused on business domain feature sets. There are other Git Workflows, like the Git Forking Workflow, as well as the Gitflow Workflow, that are repo-focused and can leverage the Git Feature Branch Workflow in order to manage their branching models. Some key pointers to keep in mind related to the Feature Branch Workflow are:

- focused on branch patterns

- are leveraged by other repo oriented workflows

- promotes collaboration with fellow developers through pull requests and merge reviews

You can also make use of git rebase during review and merge stages to create and enforce a cohesive Git history of your feature merges.

REMOTE BRANCHES

Remote references are the references or pointers in your remote repositories, and include branches, tags, etc. You should also be able to get a full list of the remote references directly with the command "git ls-remote <remote>" or even "git remote show <remote>" for the remote branches as well as additional information. Nevertheless, the more common way used is through taking advantage of the remote-tracking branches.

Remote-tracking branches happen to be references to the state of your remote branches. They are local references that cannot be moved. Git moves them around for you whenever you conduct any network communication, to ensure that they accurately represent the current state of your remote repository. See them as bookmarks, which remind you where the branches of your remote repositories were the last time you were connected to them.

Remote-tracking branches are named using the form <remote>/<branch>. For instance, if you want to see what your master branch on the origin remote looked like as of the last time that you communicated with it, you should check the origin or master branch. If you are working on an issue with a fellow coder, and they push up a branch, you might be having your own version of that branch (with the same name), but the branch on the server shall be represented by your partner's version of it.

To understand the idea better, let's take an example. Let's assume that you have a Git server on your network at git.companyname.com. If you were to clone from it, Git's clone command will automatically name it as origin, pull down its data, create a pointer toward the master branch, and name it as "master" or "origin" locally. Git will also give you your own local master branch, which will start at the same place as the origin's master branch, so that you have something to work toward.

Just like the branch name "master" does not hold any special significance for Git, neither does the name "origin". Just as the "master" is a default name for the starting branch when you have to run the command git init, "origin" is the default name of a remote when you must run the command git clone. You will work on your local master branch, and in the meanwhile, someone else will push git.companyname.com and update the master branch. Then on, your histories will move forward differently. This means that as changes are pushed more and more often, local and remote work will diverge. Additionally, as long as you stay out of touch with your origin server, your origin/master pointer will not move.

To synchronize your work within a given remote, you will have to run the git fetch <remote> command or git fetch origin. This command will look up which server origin is (git.companyname.com), and fetches any data from it that you might not have, along with updating your local database, moving the origin/master pointer to a new, more up-to-date position.

Now, let's look at the case of having many remote servers, and what the remote branches for remote projects of that kind might look like. Let us assume that we have another internal Git server used for development by one of the coding teams. The server is located at git.team1.companyname. com. You will add it as a new remote reference to the current project that you have been working on, by running the command git remote add. You could name this remote "teamone", which could be the shortname for its URL.

Now, you should run the command git fetch teamone in order to fetch everything teamone's remote server has that you do not have yet. Because this server has a subset of data that your origin server has now, Git does not fetch any data, but simply sets a remote-tracking branch called team/ one master so as to point out the commit that teamone has in place of its master branch.

Pushing

When you have to share a branch with the other coders, you must push it up to a remote that you have access to.

Your local branches will not automatically be synchronized to the remotes that you are writing to, you shall have to explicitly push the branches that you want to share. This way, you will be able to use private branches for the work that you do not wish to share, and only push up the topic branches that you look forward to collaborating on. If there is a branch that you want to work on with others, you should push it up the same way you had pushed your first branch, through the use of the command git push <remote> <branch>.

Remember that if you are using an HTTPS URL for pushing, the Git server shall be asking you for your name as well as password for the purposes of authentication. It will be prompting you on the terminal, by default, for this information, so that the server is able to tell if you can be allowed to push. If you do not wish to type your password everytime that you have to go for a push, it is recommended that you set up a "credential cache". The simplest way to do it is to just keep it in your memory for a few minutes. Then, you should be able to easily set up by running the command "git config -- global credential. helper cache". It also becomes important to understand that when you conduct a fetch that is bringing down new remote-tracking branches, you will possess local as well as editable copies of them automatically. This means that you do not get a new branch, simply a pointer that you will not be able to modify.

Tracking Branches

To checkout a local branch from a remote-tracking branch should automatically create what is known as a "tracking branch". Additionally, the branch it tracks is known as an "upstream branch". Tracking branches are the local branches that have a direct relationship with the remote branch. If you happen to be on a tracking branch, and end up typing git pull, Git will automatically know what server it is supposed to fetch from, as well as which branch to conduct the merge in.

In general, when you clone a repository, it should automatically create a master branch that tracks the origin/master. However, if you wish, you can also set up other tracking branches, like the ones that track branches on other remotes, or the ones that do not track the master branch. If the branch name you are attempting to check out does not exist, or exactly matches a name only on one remote, Git should be able to create a tracking branch for you. If a local branch has already been created, and you wish to set it to a remote branch that you just pulled down, or wish to change the upstream branch you have been tracking, you should use the -u or --set-upstream-to option to git branch, and subsequently explicitly set it at any point of time. When you will have a tracking branch set up, you should be able to refer to its upstream branch with the @{upstream} or the @{u} shorthand. So while you are on the master branch or its tracking origin/master, you will be able to say something like git merge @{u} instead of git merge origin/master, if you so wish.

If you need to see what tracking branches you have set up, you should use the -vv option to git branch. This should list out all your local branches with more information, like which branch is tracking, and whether your local branch is behind, ahead, or both. For totally up-to-date ahead and behind numbers, you will have to fetch from all your remotes, which could be performed through the command:

```
$ git fetch --all; git branch -vv
```

Pulling

While the git fetch command should fetch all the changes on the server that you might not have yet, it shall not be able to modify your working directory in any way whatsoever. It will simply acquire the data for you, and allow you to merge it yourself. However, in most cases, post git merge, a command called git pull, which is basically the same as git fetch, is carried out. If you have a set up tracking branch, either through explicitly setting it, or via having it created for yourself through the clone or checkout commands, git pull should be able to look up what server and branch are currently being tracked by your branch, fetch from the said server, and then attempt to merge in that remote branch. Generally speaking, it is better to use fetch and merge commands directly and explicitly, as the git pull can sometimes be confusing.

Deleting the Remote Branches

Let's say that you are done with your work on a remote branch. You and your collaborators have finished their work on a particular feature, and have also merged it into your remote's master branch. You should now be able to delete a remote branch using the --delete option in the git push command.

In this chapter, we focused extensively on branches, and learnt about branching and merging, branch workflows, remote branches, etc. In the next chapter, we will be turning our attention to the utility of servers, how to get Git on servers, the server setup, and information on distributed Git and projects. Read on to learn more.

CHAPTER 5

Working with Servers

IN THIS CHAPTER

➢ Getting Git on Server

➢ Server Setup

➢ Distributed Git and Projects

In the previous chapter, we learnt about branches, how to work with branches on Git, branch workflows, branching, and merging, as well as remote branches. In this chapter, we move toward learning more about servers, how to work with them, how to get Git on server, the server set up, as well as the Distributed Git and Projects. Let's start then.

DOI: 10.1201/9781003229100-5

GETTING GIT ON SERVER

Now, we have to focus on how to set up a Git service by running these protocols on your own server. We shall be demonstrating the steps as well as the commands that are required to do simplified and basic installations on a server based on Linux, though it is also possible to run these services on Windows servers or the MacOS. The actual setup of a production server using your own infrastructure will definitely entail differences in security measures, as well as operating system tools, but this is bound to give you a general idea of what all seems to be involved.

In order to set up any sort of Git server, initially, you will have to export an existing repository into a completely bare repository, i.e. a repository that does not contain a working directory. This is generally a fairly straightforward process. In order to clone your repository for the sake of creating a fresh bare repository, you will have to run the clone command with the -- bare option. Conventionally, the bare repository directory names finish with the suffix .git. Running the clone command should be able to give you a copy of the Git Directory data in your project directory. Now, you have a Git repository by itself, sans the working directory, and can now create a directory specifically for it only.

Putting the Bare Repository on a Server

So, you have a bare copy of your repository. Now, all you have to do is put it on a server, and then set up your protocols. Let us assume that you have set up a server called git.abc.com to which you also have the Secure Shell (SSH) access, and wish to store all your Git repositories under its directory. Assuming that a directory exists on that server, you should be able to set up your new repository by copying over your bare repository. This should allow other users, who possess the SSH-based read access to the directory on that server, to be able to clone your repository. If a user happens to SSH into a server, and also has to write access to the directory, they should also automatically have the push access. Git should be able to automatically add group write permissions to a particular repository if you will run the git init command with the -- shared option. Remember that by running this command, you will not be destroying any commits, refs, etc. during the process.

We can see how easy it can be to take up a Git repository, create a bare version of it, and then place it on a server where you and your collaborators should be able to gain access through SSH. With this, you and your fellow developers should be able to collaborate on the same project. Additionally, note that this is pretty much all you need in order to be able to run a useful server on Git, to which several people have access. Just make sure that you add SSH-enabled accounts on a server, as well as stick to a bare repository somewhere that all your users have read and write access to. You should be good to go with this. Nothing else is required.

Small Setups

If you are a start-up, a small company, or are simply trying out Git in your organizational space, with only a few developers, things should hopefully be fairly simple for you. One of the most complex aspects of setting up a Git server tends to be user management. If you need some repositories to be read-only for certain users, and want read as well as write access for others, getting access and permissions tends to be a convoluted process, certainly difficult to arrange and handle.

SSH Access

If you have a server setup, to which all your developers already have the SSH access, it is usually the easiest to set up your first repository there, since it requires almost no work. If you want a more complex system of access control type permissions on your repositories, you should be able to handle them using the regular filesystem permissions of the OS of your server.

If you need to place your repositories in a server that does not have accounts for everyone on your team for whom you wish to grant the write access and whatever related permissions are needed, then you have to set up an SSH access for them. We will assume that if you happen to have a server with which this function can be achieved, then you already have an SSH server installed, and that is how you are accessing the server in the first place.

There are a few ways, with which you could give access to everyone on your team. The first is to make sure that you set up accounts for everybody, which is a fairly straight-forward task, but can actually turn out to be a pretty cumbersome process. You might not want to run adduser (or its alternative useradd), and then have to set temporary passwords for every new user. Another method that can be used is the creation of a single Git user account on your machine, asking every user who will be having write access to send you an SSH public key, and subsequently add that key to a proper, specific file in the new Git account. This will not be affecting your commit data in any way whatsoever, the SSH user you will be connecting as will not affect the commits that have been recorded. Lastly, you can also try having your SSH server authenticated from a Lightweight Directory Access Protocol (LDAP) server or some other legitimate, centralized authentication source that you might already have set up. As long as every user is able to get their shell access to the machine, any SSH authentication mechanism or methodology that you can come up with should hopefully work and serve the purpose at hand.

SERVER SETUP

Let us now walk through the setup of the SSH access from the server-side. This example will have us making use of the authorized_keys method so that we are able to get our users authenticated. We will also have to assume that we are working on a standard Linux distribution like Ubuntu. A significant amount of what has been described here can be automated via the use of the ssh-copy-id command, instead of having to manually copy or install the public keys.

First, you will have to create a Git user account as well as a .ssh directory for that particular user. Next, you will have to add the developer SSH public keys into the file authorized_keys for the availability of the Git user. Let us presume that you happen to have access to some of the trusted public keys, and have also saved them to temporary files. You will now have to append them to the Git user's file authorized_keys located in the .ssh directory. Following this, you should be able to set up an empty repository by running the command git init along with the -- bare option, which should be able to initialize your repository without really needing a working directory. This should allow anyone to push the first version of their project into the repository because they will add it as a remote, and follow it up by pushing up the branch. Do keep in mind that someone has to shell onto the machine as well as create a bare repository every single time you have to add a project. We can use gitserver as the hostname of the server onto which you had set up your Git user as well as the repository. If you have been running it internally, and you have now set Domain Name System (DNS) for gitserver in order to be able to point to that server, then you should be using the commands pretty much as you usually do. Now, others should be able to clone it as well as push changes back up quite easily. Using this method, we can quickly get a read as well as write Git server up and running for a bunch of developers. You should also note that currently, all of these users should also be able to log in to the server, as well as get a shell as a Git user. If you wish to restrict that, you shall have to change the shell to something else first.

You should be able to easily restrict the Git user account to only the Git-related activities, with the aid of a limited shell tool known as git-shell, which comes along with the Git. If you will set this as the Git user's account login shell, then that account will not be able to have a normal shell access to your server. In order to use this, make sure that you specify git-shell rather than bash or csh for that particular account's login shell. In order to do so, you first have to add the full pathname of the git-shell command, and check for if it's already not there. Now, you should be able to edit a shell for your users. Additionally, the Git user can still use the SSH connection, in order to push and pull the Git Repositories, but is not allowed to shell onto the machine. If you try to do so, you will receive a login rejection from the software. At this point of time, users should be able to use the SSH port, forwarding to be able to access any host the Git server can reach. If it is important for you to prevent that, you need to edit the authorized_keys file as well as prepare the options that you would want each key to restrict itself to. Now, the Git network commands will still be working fine, but the users shall not be able to get a shell. As per the usual output, you should also be able to set up a directory in a Git user's home directory, which should be able to customize the git-shell command for a while. For example, you shall be able to restrict the Git commands which the server will accept, or you could customize the messages that users should be able to see if they attempt to enter using SSH. You could also run git help shell if you want more information on how to customize a shell.

DISTRIBUTED GIT AND PROJECTS

Now that we have set up a remote Git repository as a focal point where all the developers should be able to share their code, and we have familiarized ourselves with the basic Git commands in a local workflow, we should now look at how we can utilize some of the distributed workflows that the Git has bestowed upon us. We will learn how to work with Git in a distributed environment as a contributor as well as an integrator. This means that we will be getting educated on how we can contribute code successfully to a particular project, making it as easy and convenient as possible for us as well as the project maintainers, along with understanding how we can maintain a project successfully while a significant number of developers are contributing.

Distributed Workflow

Unlike the Centralized Version Control Systems (VCS), the distributed system of Git allows us to be way more flexible in how our coders and developers interact as well as collaborate with each other on specific tasks that are essential for the project. In the centralized system, every developer is considered to be a node working nearly equally with a central hub. In Git, though, every developer is a potential node as well as a hub; that is to say, every developer makes code contributions to other repositories, as well as helps in maintaining the public repository from which others can base their work, and to which they can contribute. This gives us a variety of workflow opportunities for our projects as well as our teams, so we shall be delving into a few common paradigms which allow us to take advantage of the flexibility the software renders us. We will also be looking into the merits as well as the demerits of every single design; which should help you to choose which one you deem the most suitable for your purposes, or the features you could mix and match from each one.

Centralized Workflow

The centralized systems usually offer us a single kind of collaboration model, the centralized workflow. The central hub, or the repository, accepts the code, and everybody else has to synchronize their work with it. Several developers are nodes, i.e. the consumers of that hub, and are expected to synchronize with that centralized location. This means that if there are two developers both cloning from the hub as well as making changes as they deem fit, the first developer who will push their changes back will manage to do so without facing any problem. The second developer, however, will have to merge the first one's work before pushing the changes up, so that he does not overwrite the changes incorporated by the first developer. This concept holds true for Git, for Subversion, or for any other Centralized VCS, and this model works perfectly well in Git, even though it is not a Centralized VCS as such. If you happen to be used to and comfortable with a centralized workflow in your organization or as part of your team, you should easily be able to continue using that kind of a workflow, with the software of Git. Just set up a single repository, and give push access to all the members of your team; Git will make sure that your users are unable to overwrite each other.

Let's take an example to understand this concept better. Two developers, A and B, started working on a project at the same time. A was able to finish his changes first, and subsequently pushed them to the server. This was followed by B trying to push her changes, but the server ended up rejecting them. B is informed that she is trying to push the non-fast-forward changes, so she will not be able to do so until she completes her fetches, and follows it up by merging. Many developers find this kind of a workflow very attractive, because it happens to be a paradigm that many seem to be familiar and comfortable with. Additionally, this kind of workflow is not merely limited to small teams. Through Git's branching model, it should be possible for hundreds of developers to be able to successfully work on one project via the use of dozens of branches simultaneously.

Integrator-Manager Workflow

Since Git allows you to have several remote repositories, it is also possible to have a kind of a workflow where each and every developer will have access to their own public repository as well as the read access to those of others who are working as part of the same team. This situation can often include a canonical repository that is supposed to represent the "official" project. In order to contribute to that project, you will have to create your own public clone of the project, and subsequently push your changes to it. Then, you will have to send a request to the maintainer of the main project, so that you can pull in the changes you have made. The maintainer then, should be able to add your repository as a remote, ensure testing your changes locally, merging them into their respective branches, and then pushing them back to their repository. To reiterate, all the steps involved in the Integration-Manager Workflow in a chronological order are:

- The project maintainer will push to their public repository.

- A contributor will clone that repository and make all the necessary changes.

- The contributor will push to their own public copy.

- The contributor will send the maintainer an email, asking them to pull all the changes made.

- The maintainer will add the contributor's repository as a remote and conduct the merge locally.

- The maintainer will push the merged changes to the main repository.

The Integration-Manager Workflow is a fairly common workflow in hub-based tools like GitLab or GitHub, where it is quite easy to fork out a project, and push your changes to the fork, so that everyone is able to see it. One of the most significant advantages of this kind of workflow is that you can continue to work, while the maintainer of the main repository should be able to pull in your changes at any point of time. Contributors do not even need to wait for the main project to incorporate their changes, each party has the freedom to work at its own pace.

Dictator and Lieutenants Workflow

This is a kind of a multiple-repository workflow. It is generally used for huge projects with hundreds and hundreds of collaborators; a famous example being the Linux kernel. Many integration managers are supposed to be in charge of certain components of the repository. They are known as lieutenants. All the lieutenants themselves have one integration manager, who is known as a benevolent dictator. For example, Junio Hamano is the benevolent dictator as well as the maintainer of Git, who also has the final say on the proposed changes for the central code. The benevolent dictator is supposed to push from their own directory to a reference repository, from which all the coding collaborators will have to pull. So, the entire process in the Benevolent dictator workflow tends to look something like this:

- Regular developers work on their respective topic branches, and later rebase their work on top of the master. The master branch belongs to the reference repository to which the dictator is supposed to push.

- Lieutenants merge the topic branches of the developers into their master branch.

- The lieutenants' master branches are merged into the dictator's master branch by him.

- The dictator pushes the master branch into the reference repository so that the other developers can rebase from it.

This kind of workflow, however, is not very common. Nevertheless, it can be useful for massive projects, or in immensely hierarchical environments. This workflow also allows the project leader, or the dictator, to delegate a lot of the work, as well as collect large subsets of code at numerous points, before eventually integrating them.

So, these are some of the most-used workflows, which are possible in a distributed system like Git. But many other variations are possible, and you can employ a diverse range of features and spend proper time for research and exploration, before figuring out what kind of workflow will best suit your real-world needs.

Contributing to Projects

It is difficult to wax eloquent on how you could be able to contribute to a particular project, since there are numerous variations on how one could go about achieving their objectives. Since Git is highly flexible, people tend to work together in a variety of ways, and it can be highly problematic to opine upon how one should contribute, since every project is a bit different. Some of the variables that are involved in project development are the active contributor count, commit access, chosen workflow, as well as the external contribution method. Let's delve into each of these factors for our better understanding.

The first variable is the active contributor count, i.e. how many contributors will be actively writing code for this project, and how often? In many cases, you will have two or three developers with only a few commits a day, or possibly even less for projects that are somewhat dormant. For bigger organizations and massive projects, the number of active developers could go up to thousands, with hundreds and thousands of commits being made per day. This is a very, very important aspect because, with more developers coming on board, you will run into more and more issues involving making sure that your code is being applied cleanly and can be easily merged together. Changes that you submit might be rendered obsolete, or heavily broken, due to the work that was being merged when you were working, or waiting for your changes to be approved or implemented. You will have to consistently ensure that your commits are valid, and your code is regularly updated.

The next factor is the workflow that is being used for the project. Is it centralized, with every developer given equal write access to the central codeline? Will you be having a maintainer or an integration manager who will be checking all of the patches? Are all the patches being peer-reviewed as well as approved? Will you be involved in that process? Is there a lieutenant system in place, and would you have to submit your work to the lieutenants first?

The next factor is the commit access. The workflow needed in order to be able to contribute to a project is way different depending on whether and what kind of access you have to a particular project. If you have not been given the write access, what exactly is the nature and form of the contributed work that you shall have to submit? Does this involve a policy? How much work are you expected to contribute at a time? How often will you have to contribute?

All of these questions have to be pondered upon as well as considered, since they will affect how you can contribute effectively to a project, and what workflows are preferred by you as well as available to you.

Commit Guidelines

First and foremost, a quick note about commit messages: if you have a good guideline for creating commits, then stick to it, as it makes working with Git as well as collaborating with other developers a significantly better experience. The Git project also provides a document laying down a number of effective tips for creating commits from which you could send out patches.

First and foremost, your submissions must not contain any whitespace errors. Git gives you a fairly easy way to check for this issue. Before you commit, you will have to run the command git diff --check, which will be able to identify the possible whitespace errors and list them out for you as well. If you will run this command before doing your commits, you will be able to tell if there are whitespace issues in your code that are bound to annoy your fellow developers.

Next, you should try to make each commit a logically separated changeset. Additionally, try to make your changes brief as well as digestible. Do not code for a couple of days on five separate issues, and then submit it all as one huge commit. Even if you do not wish to commit immediately, make sure that you utilize the staging area meaningfully, splitting your work into at least one commit per issue, with every commit made accompanied by a useful and concise message explaining the changes you have chosen to make. If some changes are modifying the same file, use the command git add --patch in order to partially stage the files (comes under the ambit of Interactive Staging). At the tip of the branch, the project snapshot remains identical, whether you commit once or thrice, as long as your changes have been added at some point, so attempt to make things easier for your fellow developers when they shall have to review the changes that you have made. This approach will also make it easier if you wish to pull out or revert your changesets, if you wish to do so later. So, make sure that you stage files in an interactive fashion to craft a clean as well as an understandable history for your commits before sending out your work to somebody else.

Next, let's discuss the commit message. Make a habit of drafting out quality commit messages that make collaboration on Git a highly smooth and convenient process. The general rule goes that you should start out with a single line that is not more than 50 characters, and is able to describe the changeset in a concise as well as meaningful way, followed by a single blank line, which is then followed by a more detailed explanation of the changeset. The Git project also asks that your detailed explanation must contain the motivation for the change that you made, and contrast the implementation now with its erstwhile behavior. Additionally, your commit message should necessarily be drafted as imperatives, i.e. write "Fix bug" not "Fixed the bug" or "Will Fix the Bug". This convention is used to match up with the commit messages that are generated by the commands git merge as well as git revert. You should try wrapping up the explanatory text in around 72 odd characters. For better understanding, think of the first line as a Subject Line in an email, whereas the rest of the text is the email body. The blank space between the two lines is of critical importance, unless of course, you choose to do away with the second line altogether. Tools like Rebase will get confused in absence of the required blank space. Bullet points can be used, if you wish to do so. Typically, a hyphen or an asterisk is used in place of the bullet, followed by a single space, with blanks between lines, as has been mentioned previously as well. You must also make use of a hanging indent.

If you will keep all these pointers in mind while writing your commit messages, things should be much easier for you and your collaborators as you work together for the success of your project. The Git project also contains good, well-formatted commit messages. You should try running the command git log -- no-merges, and be able to see what a well-formatted commit history for a project should look like.

With this, we reach the end of this chapter. In this chapter, we discussed how we can work with servers, from getting Git on a server and the Server Setup to Distributed Git & Projects. In the next chapter, we jump to GitHub, its history, how to use it, different kinds of accounts, etc. To know more, read on.

CHAPTER 6

GitHub

IN THIS CHAPTER

➢ What is GitHub

➢ History of GitHub

➢ How to use GitHub

➢ Different types of Accounts

In the previous chapter, we focused on servers, how to manage work on Git using them, the Server Setup, Distributed Git and Projects, etc. In this chapter, we will move to an associated, yet fresh topic, GitHub, with a focus on its history, use, other linked issues, etc.

WHAT IS GITHUB?

I have seen some truly revolutionary actions happen in communities on GitHub. People are collaborating

DOI: 10.1201/9781003229100-6

on code but they're also having foundational con-
versations on best practices and how software,
as a whole, is built. More and more, GitHub is an
Internet archive. It's a deeply social and critical
piece of our infrastructure.

MIKHAEL GLUKHOVSKY
Developer, Stripe

GitHub, Inc. is an Internet Hosting provider for software
development as well as version control using Git. It offers
source code management (SCM) as well as the distributed version control functionality provided by Git, apart
from the other features of its own. It provides collaboration features like feature requests, task management, bug
tracking, continuous integration, wikis, as well as access
control for different projects that you might choose to
undertake. With its headquarters in California, it has been

a subsidiary of Microsoft, since the multinational technology corporation acquired it in 2018. Usually, it is utilized to host open-source projects. GitHub claims to have more than 190 million repositories, with at least 28 million public repositories included in that number, as well as over 40 million users, as of January 2020. As of April 2020, it is recognized as the largest source code host. A significant percentage of the existing Git repositories are hosted on GitHub, and several open-source projects make use of the provider for Git Hosting, code review, issue tracking, and many other things. So while it might not be a direct part of the Git project, there is a very high chance that you will want to or have to interact with GitHub at some point of time, if you continue to operate on Git professionally.

Now, we will learn about how we can use GitHub professionally, as well as effectively. We will delve into how we can sign up for as well as manage an account, the creation and use of Git repositories, common workflows that should help you in contributing to projects, along with accepting contributions to yours, the programmatic interface of GitHub, as well as a number of other tips that should make your life easier.

Account Set Up and Configuration

The first thing you should be doing is to set up a free user account. Just visit github.com, choose a username that has not been already taken, give an email address as well as password, and follow it up by clicking on the big green "Sign Up for GitHub" button.

After passing through the GitHub sign-up form, the next thing you should see is the pricing page for the upgraded plans, but it will be better to ignore this for now, as a learner and a beginner. GitHub will also send you an email in order to be able to verify the address you provided. It is immensely important that you do not skip this step and complete the verification process in full and proper. Following this, you should click the Octocat logo at the top-left of the screen, which should be able to take you to the dashboard page of your account. You are now all set to use GitHub.

Notably, GitHub provides almost all its functions in the free accounts only, except for some advanced features. GitHub's paid services include advanced features and tools, as well as higher limits for the free services. There are three plans that GitHub offers: Free, Team, and Enterprise. The Free plan provides the basic services for individuals as well as organizations. They include:

- Unlimited public as well as private repositories.

- 2000 automation minutes per month (free for the public repositories).

- New issues as well as projects (with limited beta).

- 500 MB package storage (this is free for public repositories).

- Community support.

The Team package, meant for advanced collaboration between individuals and organizations, provides everything available in the Free pack as well as:

- Protected Branches.

- Ability to draft pull requests.

- Several reviewers fpr pull requests.

- Required reviewers.

- Code owners.

- 3000 automation minutes per month (this is free for public repositories).

- Pages and Wikis.

- 2 GB package storage (this is free for public repositories).

- Web-based support.

The Enterprise Package, meant for security, compliance, as well as flexible deployment, will offer you everything provided by the Team package and other benefits like:

- Automatic security as well as version updates.

- Advanced Auditing.

- Security Assertion Markup Language (SAML) single sign-on. This feature is used for the purposes of online security, wherein you should be able to access several web applications using a single set of login credentials.

- GitHub Connect.

- 50 GB of packages storage (this is free for public repositories).

- 50,000 automation minutes per month (this is free for public repositories).

Exclusive Add-Ons like:

- Premium Support.

- Token, secret, as well as code scanning.

While the free package, as the name would suggest, is free of cost, the Team and the Enterprise Packages should cost you $4 and $21 per user per month, respectively.

SSH Access

As of now, you can absolutely connect with the Git repositories, using the https://protocol. You will have to authenticate with your username and password that you just used for the setup process. However, in order to simply clone public projects, you will not even have to sign up, the account comes into play only if we want to fork projects or push toward our forks. If you want to use the Secure Shell (SSH) Remotes, you might need to configure a public key. If you happen to not have one, you might want to get it generated. The process to get this done is similar across all Operating Systems. First, make sure that you already do not have one. Usually, by default, a user's SSH keys are stored in that user's ~/ .ssh directory. You should also be able to see if you have a key already by going to that directory and asking for its contents to be listed. If you do not find your private key, as well as an associated public key, or if you do not even have a. ssh directory, you should be able to create them by running a program known as ssh-keygen, provided by the SSH package on Linux/macOS systems and coming with Git for the Windows.

Now, open your account settings, by clicking on the settings icon at the top-right of the window. Then select the "SSH Keys" section on the left-hand side. Then, click on the "Add an SSH key" button, give a name to your key, paste the contents of the public key into the text area, and press "Add Key". Note that you should name your SSH key something that you will be able to remember later on. You can name each of the keys like "Work Account", "Work Laptop", etc. since it will allow you to revoke a key later, as you will easily be able to tell what exactly you are looking for.

Your Avatar

Next, if you wish to do so, you should replace the avatar that has been generated for you with an image of your choice. First, go to the tab "Profile" (it is located above the SSH keys tab) and press on "Upload new picture". Crop the image as you deem fit, and click on the button "Set new profile picture". Now, wherever you will interact on the site, people will be able to see your avatar as well as your username. If you had earlier uploaded an avatar to the highly popular Gravatar service (usually used for WordPress accounts), that avatar shall be used by default, and you will not have to perform this step at all.

Email Addresses

Your email address is of particular importance on GitHub. This is because GitHub maps your Git commits to your user through the use of your email ID. If you happen to use multiple email addresses while doing your commits and you want to ensure that GitHub links them up properly, you will have to add all the email addresses you have used or intend to use in the future to the Emails tab in the Admin section. In the "Add Email Addresses" section, we should be able to see some of the states that are possible. The topmost address is usually the one that is verified and set as your primary address. This means that all the notifications and receipts that GitHub wants to send to you will be sent out at this address. The second address should also hopefully be verified, and so you could set it as your primary if you wish to do so. If you have also decided to use an unverified email address, that is perfectly alright, but GitHub will not allow you to make it your primary email address, even if you wish to do so. If GitHub shall see any of these email addresses in your commit messages in any repository of the site, they will automatically be linked to you/your user from now onward.

Two-Factor Authentication

Lastly, for additional security, you should certainly set up your Two-Factor Authentication (2FA). 2FA is a kind of an authentication mechanism that has been becoming more and more popular recently in order to mitigate the risk of your account becoming compromised if your password is somehow stolen. Turn it on and GitHub will ask you for two separate methods of authentication, so that if one of them happens to get compromised, some attacker will not be able to gain access to your account.

You should be able to find the 2FA set-up under the "Security" Tab of your account settings. First, click on the "Set up two-factor authentication" button. This should be able to take you to a configuration page where you should choose to use a phone app in order to generate your secondary code, i.e. a "time based one-time password"), or you could ask GitHub to reach out to you by sending you a code via SMS each time you have to log in.

After you make a choice on what method you prefer as well as follow the given instructions for setting up 2FA, your account should definitely be a little more secure, and you will have to provide a code along with your password whenever you feel the need to login to GitHub, to ensure that your account is not jeopardized due to security reasons.

HISTORY OF GITHUB

The development of GitHub.com platform started on October 19, 2007. The official website was launched in the April 2008 by Chris Wanstrath, Tom Preseten-Werner, P.J. Hyett, as well as Scott Chacon after it had been available for a few months as a beta release. GitHub, Inc. was initially supposed to be a flat organization, with no middle managers whatsoever. The company adopted the principle of self-management, wherein every worker had to play a part of the manager for her/himself. Additionally, GitHub's employees could choose to work on the projects that they were interested in (open allocation), even though the salaries were determined by the chief executive. In 2014 eventually, the organization introduced a layer of middle-management for better efficiency in handling its affairs.

GitHub started out as a bootstrapped start-up business, which in its early years managed to generate sufficient revenue in order to be funded solely by the three co-founders, who were also able to take on employees. Four years after the company began, Andreessen Horowitz gave it an investment of hundred million dollars in venture capital.

July 2015 saw GitHub raising another $250 million worth of venture capital in a round of B series. The investors this time around were Sequoia Capital, Andreessen Horowitz, Thrive Capital, as well as other venture capital funds. By July 2021, GitHub had made $650 million, according to the Annual Recurring Revenue. GitHub had been developed by Chris Wanstrath, P.J. Hyett, Tom Preseten-Werner, as well as Scott Chacon using Ruby on Rails, a server-side web application framework written in the programming language Ruby under the MIT License. While its primary service started in February 2008, the company itself has existed since 2007, with its main office located in San Francisco, California. On February 24, 2009, then in its second year, the company announced that within the first year of being online, it had accumulated more than 46,000 public repositories, 17,000 among them having been created in the previous month. At that point of time, around 6200 repositories were being forked at least once, while 4600 had already been merged. In the same year, GitHub's official site was harnessed by more than 100,000 users, and had also grown to host 90,000 distinct public repositories, 12,000 of which had been forked at least once, for a sum total of 135,000 repositories. By 2010, GitHub was hosting over a million repositories. A year later, this number had doubled. ReadWriteWeb, a web technology blog reported that GitHub was able to even surpass other SCM companies like SourceForge and GoogleCode as far as the total number of commits made from the duration of January to May 2011 were concerned. On the date of January 16, 2013, GitHub officially passed the three million users mark, and was subsequently hosting more than five million repositories. By the end of the same year, the number of total repositories had again doubled, with the number now reaching ten million. 2012 saw GitHub raising $100 million worth of funds from Andreessen Horowitz with a total valuation of $750 million. On July 29, 2015, it got reported that GitHub had raised a funding of $250 million in a round that had been led by Sequoia Capital, an American venture capital firm. The other investors of that round had been Andreessen Horowitz, Institutional Venture Partners (IVP), as well as Thrive Capital, known for mostly investing in technology companies. The round had valued the company at approximately $2 billion. The year 2015 saw GitHub open its first office outside the United States, in Tokyo, Japan. In 2016, the company made an appearance on the Forbes Cloud 100 list at the rank of 14. However, it hasn't managed to make an appearance since. On February 28, 2018, the company fell victim to the third-biggest distributed denial-of-service attack (DDoS) in history, with its incoming traffic reaching a peak of around 1.35 terabytes each second. On June 19, 2018, GitHub expanded GitHub Education by offering free education bundles to schools.

Acquired by Microsoft

From 2012 onward, Microsoft became a crucial customer as well as a significant user of GitHub, utilizing its services to be able to host open-source projects as well as development tools like Chakra Core, .NET Core, PowerShell, MS Build, Visual Studio Code, Power Toys, Windows Terminal, Windows Calculator, as well as a bulk of its product documentation (now found on Microsoft Docs). On June 4, 2018, Microsoft expressed its intent to acquire

GitHub for $7.5 billion. The deal was closed on October 26, 2018. GitHub, nevertheless, still continues to operate independently as a platform, community, as well as a business. Under Microsoft, the service came under the leadership of Xamarin's Nat Friedman, reporting to the Executive Vice-President of Microsoft Cloud & AI, Scott Guthrie. The GitHub CEO Chris Wanstrath was kept as a "technical fellow," with him reporting to Guthrie as well. However, this acquisition too had its fair share of controversies. Developers like Kyle Simpson, author as well as JavaScript trainer, and Rafael Laguna, CEO, Open-Xchange (a web-oriented communication, collaboration, as well as office productivity software suite) expressed their concerns and uneasiness over Microsoft's purchase, citing Microsoft's handling, or mishandling of previous purchases, like Nokia's mobile business, Skype, etc.

This acquisition was in line with the business strategy of the corporation under CEO Satya Nadella, which saw a greater emphasis being put on the cloud computing services, as well as the contributions to and the development of open-source software. In 2016, Microsoft was on the top of the list of ten different organizations with the most open-source contributors on GitHub. Harvard Business Review asserted that Microsoft intending to acquire GitHub was merely to get access to its user base, which it could use as a loss leader, in order to encourage the use of its other development services and products. The concerns expressed over GitHub's sale seemed to benefit its competitors, at least for a while. GitLab, a commercial open-source software that runs a hosted service version control system, Bitbucket (owned by Atlassian), as well as SourceForge (owned by BizX) reported a bolstered interest from the market, with spikes in new users who intended to migrate their projects from GitHub to their respective services. GitHub acquired Semmle, a code analysis tool in September 2019. February 2020 saw GitHub being launched in India with much fanfare under the name GitHub India Private Limited. Later on, GitHub went on to acquire npm, a JavaScript packaging vendor, for an undisclosed amount of money, closing the deal on April 15, 2020. In July 2020, the GitHub Archive Program was founded, in order to archive its open-source code for perpetuity.

Mascot

GitHub's mascot is an "octocat," an anthropomorphized creature with five octopus-like arms. This character was the brainchild of graphic designer Simon Oxley as clip art that he intended to sell on iStock, an online royalty-free, international microstock photography provider based in Canada. GitHub was interested in Oxley's work after Twitter chose a bird that he designed for their own logo. The illustration that GitHub eventually chose was a character that Oxley had named "Octopuss". Since GitHub wanted Octopuss as their logo (a use that the iStock license does not permit), they negotiated with Oxley in order to be able to buy the exclusive rights of the image. GitHub rechristened Octopuss to Octocat, and trademarked the character along with this new name. Later, GitHub hired an illustrator named Cameron McEfee to adapt Octocat for different purposes on the website as well as the promotional materials; McEfee and various other GitHub users have since created hundreds and hundreds of variations of the character, which are available on the GitHub Octodex.

So, basically while there were many prospective preachers who could have spread the open-source religion, whether it was Google Code or SourceForge, GitHub eventually trumped them all. When Git was released in 2005, open-source was experiencing something akin to a renaissance. Interest in as well as a desire to adopt Linux was strong. The first Web 2.0 applications were beginning to emerge. Several companies preferred to migrate their tech stacks to the available open-source servers. Although Git made collaborating on open-source projects efficient as well as effortless by introducing the concept of forking, there was one thing that Git couldn't do: help coders find these open-source projects. A lot of programmers had been working on many exciting open-source projects, but to find them in the first place was a very difficult task.

It is this lacuna that GitHub set out to fill, and managed to do so in time, passing with flying colors. When Hyett and Wanstrath began working on what ultimately became GitHub in 2007, both of them were working as programmers for a tech website called CNET (short for Computer Network). Both liked the development framework that was offered by Ruby on Rails. While holding their day jobs, Hyett and Wanstrath ended up developing several suggestions as well as improvements for the codebase of their favorite Rails. However, no one was interested in looking at their code, at least not at that point of time. As was the standard procedure for most open-source projects at that time, Rails' codebase was kept in check by a small as well as tight-knit group of coders who were managing the contributions that had been made to the main code manually. They were the project gatekeepers, and even if one of them had ended up liking the work done by Hyett and Wanstrath, merging patches for real was not a straightforward process at all. On some level, making contributions to Rails became a matter of who you knew, and rather than what you knew. It is serendipitous that their enduring contribution would be GitHub, an essential provider tool for Git today, because Torvalds' conception of Git, too, was in many ways rooted in ideas like the democratization of code development, as well as allowing developers to collaborate on projects with minimal gatekeeping involved. Nevertheless, despite the significant convenience that Git ended up giving developers, there was also an incredible lack of collaborative tools for it. Sharing code between two developers in itself was an arduous process. Software developers would tend to email patches between themselves until the changes in code would be able to resolve whatever issue had been cropping up. It becomes easy to see why something like GitHub was so sorely needed. Other developments were also being offered for the improvement of Git. The software used to primarily rely on the Command Line Interface, but the GUI too was soon developed for it. Preston-Werner, a Ruby programmer from the Bay area, started working on a project known as "Grit", conceived of as a tool that would allow the coders to be able to access Git repositories in an object-oriented manner using the language Ruby on Rails. His objective was clear: to create a place that would be able to host entire code libraries, and where programmers would be able to work on code projects more collaboratively, along with learning more about Git as well as its potential uses. As Preston-Werner conceived it, it would be a "Git hub".

HOW TO USE GITHUB

GitHub is a web-based platform that is used for version control. Git, on the other hand, simplifies the process of working with other developers, fostering the spirit as well as the practical possibilities of collaboration. Team members are supposed to work on their respective file, and later merge the changes into the master branch of the project. Skills pertaining to Git as well as GitHub have slowly been promoted from preferred skills to must-have skills for multiple job roles.

How to Create a Repository on GitHub?

A repository is a storage space for your product. The repository can be local, i.e. available on a folder in your computer, or it could be a storage space provided by an online host, like GitHub. You should be able to keep your code files, images, text files, or any other kind of a file in a repository. You will require a GitHub repository for your project, when you are done making changes to your files, and they are now prepared to be uploaded. The GitHub repository will thus act as your remote repository. In order to create a repository on GitHub, follow the given steps:

- Visit the link GitHub.com. Fill the Sign-Up form, and press on the button "Sign up for GitHub".

- Click on the option "Start a new project".

- Enter a name for your repository, and follow it up by clicking on the button "Create Repository". You are also allowed to give a description of your repository, though this step is absolutely optional.

Now, you shall be able to notice that by default, a GitHub repository is public, which means that anyone should be able to see the contents of your repository/project. In the case of a private repository, which comes as part of the paid version of GitHub, you should be able to choose the entities to whom you will allow access to your repository as well as its contents. Also, you should be able to initialize your repository through a README file. The README file contains the description of your file, and once you have checked this box, it should be the first file in your repository. Now that your repository has been successfully created, you are ready to make commits, push, pull, and perform all the necessary operations. Now, we move on to understanding branching in GitHub.

Create Branches

Branches will help you in working on multiple versions of a repository at a particular time. You might want to add a new feature (still in the development phase), but are unsure if whether making changes to the main codeline will be worth it. Git Branching to the rescue! Branches should allow you to move back and forth between different versions of your project. In the aforementioned scenario, you will be well-advised to fork out a branch and test the new feature without any adverse effects on the main branch. Once your changes are tried, tested, and approved, you can merge the changes from the new branch to the main branch. Here, the main branch refers to the master branch, present in your repository by default.

In order to create a new branch in GitHub, you will have to follow the provided set of instructions:

- Click on the drop-down option of "Branch: master".

- Just as you click on the branch, you will be able to find an existing branch, or you shall have to create one. Let's say we create a branch and name it "readme-changes". After creating the new branch, you shall have two branches in your repository, the read-me, i.e. the master branch, as well as the branch readme-changes. The new branch is a mere clone of the master branch. To make it different, you will have to make changes via several operations that we will now delve into.

Making Commits

Committing will save changes to your file. A commit should ideally be accompanied by a message justifying and explaining the changes that have been made. The commit message is not compulsory, yet is strongly recommended by nearly all organizations, for purposes of differentiation, and helping the collaborators understand the history of a file as well as the changes made. In order to make your first commit on GitHub, follow the given steps in a chronological order:

- Click on the "readme-changes" file that we created in the last section.

- Press on "Edit" or a pencil icon which you should be able to find in the right-most corner of this file.

- Once you click on it, an editor will open where you should be able to type in the changes required.

- Write a commit message identifying the changes made. (Recollect the line-wise format: describe changes-blank-explanation of changes).

- Click on "Commit Changes" in the end.

Pull Command

Pull command is one of the most important commands in GitHub. It will inform you regarding the changes made to a file, request your fellow contributors to view it, and merge it with the master branch as well. Once a commit has been made, anyone should be able to pull the file, and initiate a discussion on the change/s. Once the iteration process is complete, the file/s can be merged. If there are any conflicts between the different changesets, they will have to be resolved in order to complete the merge. Now, let us go through the various steps involved in order to conduct a pull request on GitHub:

- Click on the "Pull Requests" tab.

- Press on "New Pull Request".

- After clicking on the pull request, select the branch and click on the file to be able to view the changes between the two files that are present in our repository.

- Click on "Create Pull Request".

- Enter the title, description of your changes, followed up by clicking on "Create pull request".

Merge Command

Through the use of the Merge command, we merge the changes made into the master branch. To use the Merge command on GitHub, follow these steps in a chronological order:

- Click on the "Merge pull request" to merge your changes into the master branch.

- Click on "Confirm Merge".

- You should be able to delete the branch once all of its changes have been incorporated, and if there were no conflicts.

Cloning and Forking GitHub Repository

Cloning is essential so that we can download codes from remote repositories, and make suitable changes to them using commits. To clone on GitHub, you simply need to press the green-colored button that contains the text "Clone or Download".

Forking is done to create a new branch, and subsequently make changes to the central codeline, while usually focusing on one particular feature, the new branch created is generally referred to as a feature branch. A few pointers that you need to be keep in mind about Forking:

- Changes made to the original repository will get reflected back to the forked repository.

- If you will make changes in a forked repository, it shall not be getting reflected to the original repository until and unless you call for a pull request.

In order to be able to fork a repository in GitHub, make sure that you follow the given sequence of steps:

- Go to the Explore section and make a search on the public repositories.

- You should open a repository, and you will be able to find a number besides the "Fork" button telling you how many times it has previously been forked. Click on "fork".

After you click on Fork, it will take some time for the software to give you your own local version of the public repository. Once done, you will be able to notice the name of that particular repository under your account. Congratulations! You have successfully managed to fork out an existing repository under your own account on GitHub.

DIFFERENT TYPES OF ACCOUNTS

On GitHub, your user account is your identity for all practical purposes. Your user account is allowed to be a member of as many organizations as you want to be affiliated with. Organizations mostly belong to the enterprise accounts.

Personal User Accounts

Every person who will use GitHub will have a personal account, which will include:

- Limitless private as well as public repositories with GitHub free.

- No limit on collaborators (GitHub Free).

- Supplementary features for the private repositories with GitHub Pro.

- Can collaborate to work on repositories.

Remember that you are allowed to use a single account for multiple purposes, for personal use as well as business purposes. It is generally recommended to avoid creating multiple accounts because of the problems that might ensue. Nevertheless, GitHub does provide you the facility to be able to merge several user accounts together. Furthermore, while the GitHub user accounts are intended to be used by human beings, you could also give one to a robot, like a continuous integration bot, if you need to.

Organization Accounts

Organization Accounts are defined as shared accounts where large groups of people are able to collaborate across multiple projects at the same time. Administrators or the owners tend to manage the access of various members to an organization's data as well as projects through a host of administrative features as well as robust, sophisticated security. Various features that you will be able to find in Organization accounts are:

- Unlimited membership with a plethora of roles which will grant you different levels of access to an organization as well as its data.

- An ability to give their members a gamut of access permissions to their organization's repositories.

- Nested teams which will reflect your group or company's structure with cascading access mentions as well as permissions.

- The ability for the owners of an organization to check the 2FA status of the members of the account/ organization.

- The option to make the 2FA mandatory for all the members of the project.

You should be able to make use of organization accounts for free through GitHub Free. The facilities include unlimited repositories with all the features, unlimited collaborators to work on projects with, as well as unlimited private repositories with limited features. For more features, like better support coverage, sophisticated user authentication as well as management, you should upgrade to GitHub Team or GitHub Enterprise Cloud. If you use the latter, in particular, you will have the option to purchase the license for GitHub Advanced Security and use the features of private repositories.

Enterprise Accounts

Through enterprise accounts, you should be able to manage billing as well as policy for multiple GitHub.com organizations at the same time. Enterprise accounts are usually available with GitHub Enterprise Cloud as well as GitHub Enterprise Server.

With this, we have come to the end of this chapter on GitHub. In this chapter, we talked about what GitHub is, its history, different ways of using GitHub, as well as the different types of accounts that are available on GitHub. com. In the next chapter, we will move to GitLab, and learn about what it is, its history, how to use it, and other details on it. Read on to know more.

CHAPTER 7

GitLab

IN THIS CHAPTER

➤ What is GitLab

➤ History of GitLab

➤ How to use GitLab

➤ Free and Enterprise accounts

In the previous chapter, we focused our mental faculties on GitHub, what it was, its history, how to use it, different kinds of accounts it offers, etc. With this chapter, we move on to GitLab, keeping our concerns in similar directions. So, let's begin.

WHAT IS GITLAB

GitLab is a web-oriented DevOps tool that should be able to provide you with a Git repository manager and features pertaining to continuous integration and deployment,

DOI: 10.1201/9781003229100-7

providing wiki, issue-tracking, etc. by making use of an open-source license that was developed by Git Inc. DevOps here refers to a compendium of practices that are able to combine software development (Dev) with IT operations (Ops). The chief aim of DevOps is to reduce a system's development life cycle, as well as provide continuous delivery of quality software. DevOps conceptually is often complemented by the idea of Agile software development, which is also the source of several ideas that DevOps continues to grapple with. As a project, GitLab was created and developed by Dmitriy Zaporozhets and Valery Sizov. Its code was originally written using Ruby on Rails, as well as some of the later parts in Go, a statically typed, compiled programming language, that was designed at Google. The code was supposed to work to provide a source code management (SCM) solution to improve the process of collaboration between a software development team. Later, its evolution took it toward becoming an integrated solution for the software development life cycle, and eventually to the entire DevOps life cycle. The latest technology stack of the tool includes Ruby on Rails, Go, as well as Vue.js, an open-source JavaScript framework utilized for building single-page applications as well as user interfaces. GitLab follows the model of open-core development, wherein the core functionality had been released under MIT's open-source license, while the supplementary features of functionality, like multiple issue assignees, code owners, dependency scanning, as well as insights, are to be kept under the ambit of a proprietary license. GitLab's services are only available in the English language, while its headquarters are located in San Francisco, California,

United States. Its services are available worldwide, and it is owned by GitLab Inc. The names of the founders are Sytse "Sid" Sijbrandij, Dmitriy Zaporozhets, and Valery Sizov, while the key members of the organization include Sijbrandij as CEO and Co-Founder, and Zaporozhets and Sizov as co-founders. The total revenue generated by the software company amounted to 150 million American dollars in 2020, while the total number of employees are 1419. The URL for the service is gitlab.com, and the registration in order to be able to avail the service launched in 2014 is optional.

HISTORY OF GITLAB

In 2011, Dmitriy Zaporozhets was in need of a good tool in order to be able to collaborate with his team. He was in want of something that was efficient as well as enjoyable so he could actually focus on and enjoy his work, rather than getting caught up in the tools themselves. GitLab was created by Zaporozhets from his house in Ukraine, a home without running water. The GitLab official website claims that "Dmitriy perceived not having a great collaboration tool as a bigger problem than his daily trip to the communal well." As a result, in collaboration with Valery, he began the creation of GitLab as a solution to the problem at hand. The first commit was made on October 8, 2011. The name of the company was inspired by and drawn from GitWeb, and several other products that were affiliated with Git.

In 2012, Sijbrandij came across GitLab for the first time, and felt it natural that a collaboration tool for programmers be open source, so that as many as possible could contribute to it. He was a Ruby programmer himself, so he went through the source code and was seriously impressed by the quality of the code developed, after more than 300 contributions were made in the first year of the project. He subsequently reached out to Hacker News, a social news website with computer science as well as entrepreneurship as its primary concerns, asking them if they would be interested in using GitLab.com. Hundreds of people chose to sign up for the beta version of the product. November 2012 saw Dmitriy making the first version of GitLab Continuous Integration (CI). By 2013, huge organizations that were making use of GitLab asked Sijbrandij to include the features that they were searching for, to improve the efficiency of their companies as well as the work done there. Dmitriy too decided that he wanted to work on GitLab full time. Sid and Dmitriy then teamed up and subsequently introduced the Enterprise Edition of GitLab along with the features that were being asked for by the larger organizations. This was done by splitting the product into two disparate versions: GitLab CE, i.e. Community Edition and

GitLab EE—the Enterprise Edition. At that point of time, the licenses of both stayed the same, both being free as well as open-source softwares distributed under the License of MIT.

2014 saw GitLab being officially incorporated as a limited liability corporation. In February 2014, it announced its adoption of an open-core business model. An open-core model tends to be a business model that is meant to be used for the monetization of open-source software that is produced commercially. GitLab EE was set under EE License, the source available proprietary, containing features that are not present in the CE Version. The GitLab CE Licensing Model, however, did not change, and the company continued to develop as well as support the CE Edition. GitLab EE became a restricted license; however, its source code, issues, and in particular, the merge requests stayed publicly visible. The company also continued releasing newer versions of the software every 22nd day of the month, just as it had every year before and has every year since. January 22, 2014 witnessed the release of GitLab 6.5, while the newest version by December 2014 was GitLab 7.6. Subsequently, GitLab also sent their application to Y Combinator, an American seed money startup accelerator that was launched in March 2005. At the start of 2015, almost the entire team of GitLab went to Silicon Valley so that they could participate in the Y Combinator. In July 2013, the company decided to split the product into two disparate versions: GitLab CE: Community Edition and GitLab EE: Enterprise Edition.

In March 2015, the company was able to acquire Gitorious, a competitor that was also providing services pertaining to hosting Git. Gitorious had around 822,000 registered users at that point of time. The said users were encouraged to make a shift to GitLab; the services provided by Gitorious were subsequently disbanded in June 2015. An alumnus of the Y Combinator seed accelerator program of its Winter 2015 batch, the company now managed to raise a further $1.5 million in its seed funding. Its customers by 2015 included Alibaba Group, a Chinese multinational technology company that specializes in e-commerce, Internet, retail, as well as technology, International Businesses Machine Corporation (IBM), and SpaceX, the Elon Musk-led American aerospace manufacturer, space communications as well as transportation services company with its headquarters in Hawthorne, California. A further $4 million were raised in Series A funding in September 2015 from Khosla Ventures, a venture capital firm that aims to focus on early-stage companies in domains as diverse as Internet, mobile, computing, biotechnology, silicon technology, biotechnology, healthcare, as well as clean technology sectors. The year 2016 proved to be a period of growth and the total number of people who contributed to the GitLab were more than 1000. The open-core business model of the company was also confirmed by its CEO. August Capital, and existing investors Y Combinator and Khosla Ventures, again participated in the Series B funding, leading GitLab to raise $20 million.

In January 2017, in the aftermath of a cyber attack, an administrator for a GitLab database accidentally deleted an entire production database. The issue and merge data for six hours was eliminated. Thankfully, it was eventually recovered, with the recovery process being live-streamed on YouTube. On March 15, 2017, GitLab acquired Gitter, an open-source instant messaging as well as chat room system for the users and the developers of GitLab as well as GitHub's repositories. However, it was also announced that the stated intent of GitLab was to allow for Gitter to continue as a standalone project. Furthermore, GitLab also announced that the code would be open-source and under an MIT License by June 2017. GitLab also raised $20 million in the Series C round that was led by GV (Google Ventures) as well as others. January 2018 saw GitLab acquiring Gemnasium, a service providing security scanners with alerts for the security vulnerabilities of the open-source libraries of multiple languages. Gemnasium's services were scheduled for a complete shutdown on the May 15. Gemnasium's technology as well as traits were integrated into GitLab EE as well as parts of CI/CD (Continuous Integration/Continuous Deployment). GitLab announced its integration with Google Kubernetes Engine (GKE), in order to simplify the processes of spinning up new clusters to be able to deploy applications.

May 2018 saw GNOME (an acronym for GNU Network Object Model Environment), a desktop environment with Unix-like OSs, move to GitLab with its more than 400 projects and 900 contributors. GitLab had to move from Microsoft Azure to Google Cloud Platform on August 11, 2018, thereby making its services inaccessible to the users of Cuba, Crimea, North Korea, Kenya, Iran, Sudan, and Syria, compelled due to the sanctions imposed by the Office of Foreign Assets Control of the United States. In order to be able to grapple with this issue, Framasoft, a non-profit organization, provided a Debian mirror in order to make GitLab CE available in the aforementioned countries. On August 1, 2018, GitLab began the development of Meltano, another open-source DataOps platform. ICONIQ Capital's participation in September 2018 led to GitLab raising a $100 million in the Series D-Round funding in September 2018. Later in 2018, GitLab was considered the first partly Ukrainian unicorn to be valued at more than $1 billion. 2019 saw the company raising $268 million in the Series E-Round funding initiated by ICONIQ Capital, an American investment as well as wealth management firm, and the famous finance-service company Goldman Sachs.

At that point of time, the company's value was estimated to be $2.7 billion. In 2019, SWFI reported that GitLab was expected to reach $100 million of ARR by January 2020. Today, more than 100,000 organizations as well as millions of users are making use of GitLab to meet their ends. In September, the team announced their master plan of raising more than 20 million dollars in the B Round of financing. By 2020, GitLab had more than 1200 team members in over 65 countries, making it the world's largest all-remote company before the COVID-19 pandemic struck. Every single employee of GitLab works remotely, there are no central headquarters or offices belonging to the company all over the globe. GitLab experienced 50× growth in 4 years, reaching the $100M ARR, i.e. Annual Recurring Revenue mark in the year 2020. The company's current value is $2.75 billion, and it has raised $426M till date. The company is still strongly oriented toward community contributions, with over 650 code contributions made every month from more than 2500 contributors. Due to their

DevOps platform, by August 2021, the company was able to grow to more than a million active license users as well as over thirty million registered users.

The company itself grew to more than 1400 team members in as many as 65 countries as well as regions all over the globe. It continues to support as well as educate enterprises regarding the advantages of remote work by conducting more than 60 collaborative discussions on remote work with organizations, universities, Vice-Chancellors, etc. since the pandemic started. As of 2021, GitLab has managed to expand its business to the Chinese market, has had OMERS participate in its secondary share investment, and has also managed to create Meltano, a new open source ELT platform.

HOW TO USE GITLAB

Now, we will learn in detail about the functionality of GitLab.

GitLab and SSH Keys

To recapitulate what has been established in the previous chapters, Git is a distributed Version Control System (VCS) that allows you to work locally, and subsequently share or "push" your changes to a server, so that your fellow developers as well as reviewers can see them too. In this case, that server happens to be the GitLab. GitLab utilizes the SSH (Shell) Protocol in order to be able to securely communicate with Git. When you make use of SSH keys in order to authenticate the GitLab remote server, you will not have to supply your username or password every single time.

Prerequisites

To be able to use SSH for your communication with GitLab, you will need the following:

- An open SSH client, which should come pre-installed on all kinds of devices, like MacOS, Windows 10, GNU/Linux, etc.

- An SSH version that is either 6.5 or later. The versions before this made use of MD5 signature, a hash algorithm (like SHA-1) that is usually used to check for data integrity. MD5 now is not recognized to be secure.

To be able to view the version of SSH that has been installed in your system, run the command ssh -V.

Supported SSH Key Types

If you wish to be able to communicate with GitLab, you can make use of the following SSH key types:

- **ED25519:** These keys are considered to be more secure and better performing than the RSA keys. OpenSSH 6.5 introduced these keys in 2014, and you should be able to find them on most operating systems.

- **RSA:** Generally, ED25519 is considered to be more secure than RSA. Nevertheless, if you happen to be using an RSA key, the United States Institute of Science and Technology generally recommends a key size of at least 2048 bits. The default key size will have to depend on your version of ssh-keygen. To know the details, you will have to review the man page for the command.

- **DSA:** Were deprecated in GitLab 11.0.

- **ECDSA:** The security issues pertaining to DSA apply in a similar fashion to ECDSA.

Administrators should be able to restrict which keys are to be permitted, as well as their minimal lengths.

But how to check if you have an existing SSH key pair? Follow the given steps:

- On Windows, macOS, or Linux, go see your home directory.

- Now, go to the .ssh/subdirectory. If it doesn't exist, you are either not in the home directory, or haven't ever used ssh before. In the case of the latter, you will have to generate an SSH key pair.

- Check for files in one of the following formats:

Algorithm	Public Key	Private Key
ED25519	id_ed25519.pub	id_ed25519
RSA	id_rsa.pub	id_rsa
DSA	id_dsa.pub	id_dsa
ECDSA	id_ecdsa.pub	id_ecdsa

Generating the SSH Keys

If you do not have an SSH pair of keys, you shall have to generate a new one:

- First, open a terminal.

- Type out the command ssh-keygen -t and follow it up with a key type as well as an optional comment. This comment has to be included in the .pub file that will be created. You might also want to use an email address for the comment.

- Press Enter.

- Accept the suggested filename as well as directory, unless you happen to be generating a deploy key or wish to save it in a specific directory where you have stored your other keys. You should also be able to dedicate an SSH key pair to a specific host.

- Give your passphrase.

- A confirmation should now be displayed, which includes information about where your files are stored.

A public and private key are thus generated. In the end, add the public SSH to your GitLab account, and keep your private key secure.

Configure Your SSH to Point to a Different Directory

If you forgot to save your SSH key pair in the default directory, you need to configure your SSH client so that it can point to the directory where your private key has been stored.

Steps:

- Open a terminal window and run the command eval $(ssh-agent -s)

```
ssh-add <directory to private SSHkey>
```

- Save the settings you need in the ~/.ssh/config file.

Public SSH keys have to be unique to GitLab since they will bind your account. Your SSH key should be the only identifier you have on you when you push code with SSH. The key must uniquely map to a single user.

Updating Your SSH Key Passphrase
You should be able to update the passphrase for your SSH key.

- Open a terminal and run the command

```
ssh-keygen -p -f/path/to/ssh_key
```

- When prompted, type your passphrase and press Enter.

Upgrade Your RSA Pair to a More Secure Format
If your version of OpenSSH lies between 6.5 and 7.8, you should be able to save your private RSA SSH in a better secured OpenSSH format.

- Open a terminal window and run the command:

```
ssh-keygen -o -f ~/.ssh/id_rsa
```

OR You could generate a fresh RSA key with a better encryption format using the command:

```
ssh-keygen -o -t rsa -b 4096 -C
"<comment>"
```

Adding an SSH Key to Your GitLab Account

To be able to use SSH with GitLab, you must copy your public key into your GitLab account.

- First, make sure that you copy the contents of your key file. You should be able to do this manually, or you could use a script.

- Sign in to GitLab.

- At the top bar, in the right corner, make a choice of your avatar.

- Select Preferences.

- From the left sidebar, select SSH keys.

- Within the Key box, you would have to paste the contents of your public key. If you do so manually, make sure that you are copying and pasting the entire key.

- In the Title box, you will have to type out a description, like Home Workstation or Work Laptop.

- You shall also have the option of specifying an expiration date (from GitLab 12.9 onward), though this is optional.

- Select "Add Key".

Verifying That You Can Connect

In order to verify that your SSH key was added correctly, follow the given steps:

- In GitLab.com, make sure that you are connected to the correct server, and confirm the SSH host keys using fingerprints.

- Open a terminal window and run the command:

```
ssh -T git@gitlab.example.com
```

- If connecting for the first time, ensure that you verify the authenticity of the GitLab host.

- Run the command ssh -T git@gitlab.example.com again. If you followed all the provided steps correctly, you should now receive a "Welcome to GitLab, @ username!" message.

If the Welcome message hasn't appeared, you will have to troubleshoot by running ssh in the verbose mode:

```
ssh -Tvvv git@gitlab.example.com
```

Using Different Keys for Different Repositories
You are allowed to use different keys for each repository. To do so, open a terminal window, and run the command:

```
git config core.sshCommand "ssh -o
IdentitiesOnly=Yes -i ~/.ssh/private-key-
filename-for-this-repository -F/dev/null"
```

This command will not use the SSH Agent and will also require Git 2.10 or later.

Using Different Accounts on a Single GitLab Instance
You are also allowed to use multiple accounts in order to connect to a single instance of GitLab. Let us first define what are instance domains? In the instance domains, there is a system instance, which consists of a number of

block instances, which end up forming a tree-like structure with the system instance as a root. Coming back to our central topic, what we seek to do can be achieved using the command in the previous section. However, even if you were able to set "IdentitiesOnly" to "yes", you shall not be able to sign in if there is an IdentityFile that exists outside of a host block. However, you can always assign aliases to hosts in the ~.ssh/config file.

- For hosts, use an alias like user_1/2.gitlab.com. Advanced configurations can be difficult to maintain, so these strings should be easier to comprehend when you make use of tools like git remote.

- For the IdentifyFile, use the path of the private key.

You can then use the git clone command to clone your repositories, and ensure to update a previously-cloned repository that will be aliased as an origin. Keep in mind that private as well as public keys contain sensitive data. You have to ensure that the permissions on the files make them readable to you, and yet not accessible to others.

Configure Two-Factor Authentication (2FA)

You should be able to set up two-factor authentication (2FA) for Git over SSH. The OTP verification can be done through the designated GitLab Shell Command:

```
ssh git@<hostname> 2fa_verify
```

Once the OTP gets verified, Git through SSvH operations can be utilized for a duration of 15 minutes (default setting) with the associated SSH key.

Using EGit on Eclipse

If you are using EGit, you should be able to add your SSH key to Eclipse using the following steps:

- Click on Window>Preferences in order to open the Eclipse Preference Dialog. Navigate through and expand your Network Connections option and subsequently select SSH. Make sure that your SSH2 home is configured correctly (in most cases, it is ~/.ssh) and contains your SSH 2 keys as well.

- If you don't have SSH keys, you should also be able to generate them from the second tab of this dialog called "Key Management". Make sure that you utilize a good passphrase in order to protect your private key.

- Now, upload your public SSH key to your GitLab profile settings.

Use SSH on Microsoft Windows

If you use Windows 10, you should either be using the Windows Subsystem for Linux with WSL 2 with both git as well as ssh pre-installed, or install Git for Windows to be able to use SSH through Powershell. The SSH key that is generated by WSL is never directly available for Git for Windows, and vice versa, since both have a different home directory, /home/<user> for WSL, and C:\Users\<user> for Microsoft.

You should also be able to copy over the .ssh/directory in order to be able to use the same key, or for generating a key in each particular environment. Alternative tools that can be used for this purpose include Cygwin, as well as PuttyGen.

Overriding SSH Settings on GitLab Server

GitLab is able to integrate with a system-installed SSH daemon as well as designate a user (usually named git) through whom all access requests are to be handled. Users who are able to connect with the GitLab server through SSH are identified by their SSH key instead of their username. SSH client operations that are performed on the GitLab server are executed by the software as this user. You should be able to modify this SSH configuration. For example, you should be able to specify a private SSH key for the user to be able to use to conduct the authentication requests. However, bear in mind that such a practice is discouraged since it is not supported and also contains major security risks. GitLab actually checks for this condition, and should be able to direct you to know if your server is configured in that manner. Make sure that you remove the custom configuration as soon as you are able to, since these customizations might stop working at any point of time as they are explicitly not supported.

Troubleshooting SSH Connections

When you run the command git clone, you will be prompted to provide a password. This will indicate that something is wrong with your SSH setup.

- Ensure that you generated your SSH key correctly as well as add it to your GitLab profile.

- Manually register for the private SSH key by running the command ssh-agent.

- Debug your connection by running the command ssh -Tv git@example.com. Needless to say, replace example.com with your GitLab URL.

You can also restrict the allowed SSH key technologies as well as their minimum length. The command ssh-keygen allows the users to create their RSA keys with as little as 768 bits, falling well below the recommendations from standard groups like US NIST. Some organizations that are making use of GitLab must enforce the rule of the minimum key strength, in order to ensure regulatory compliance as well as to satisfy the internal security policy. Additionally, many standard groups recommend the use of RSA, ECDSA, or even ED25519 over the much older DSA, and the administrators might need to limit the permitted SSH key algorithms.

In order to restrict the allowed SSH key technology along with the minimum key length for each technology, follow the given steps:

- At the top bar, select Menu followed by the option of Admin.

- In the left sidebar, choose Settings > General.

- Expand the section containing details on the Visibility and access controls section. If you see a restriction imposed on a specific type of key, users should not be able to upload the new SSH keys which fail to meet the prescribed requirements. The keys which won't meet it will be disabled (not removed) and the users will not be able to pull or push code using them. You will also find an icon (with the symbol of an exclamation mark) containing a restricted key in the section meant for SSH keys on your profile. Hover your cursor over the icon, and you will get the reason as to why that particular key has been restricted.

By default, the self-managed settings of the supported key types in GitLab.com are following:

- DSA SSH keys are disallowed (from GitLab 11.0).

- RSA SSH keys are allowed.

- ECDSA SSH keys are permitted.

- ED25519 SSH keys are permitted as well.

Creating a Project

In order to create a new project in GitLab, follow the given steps:

1. Find your dashboard, and in it, click on the green New project button or, you could use the plus icon found in the navigation bar. This should be able to open up the New project page.

2. Once you are on the New project page, choose whether you want to create a new blank project, use one of the available templates in order to do so, run CI/CD pipelines for external repositories, import a project from the new repository, if it is enabled for your GitLab instance, etc. If not, contact your GitLab administrator.

Creating a Group

In order to create a group, follow the provided steps:

- On the top bar, select Menu > Groups, and on the right, select "Create Group". From the left side of the search box, select the plus sign and then, click on "New Group".

- Select "Create Group".

- For the group name, you can only use alphanumeric characters, underscores, as well as emojis. The use of dashes, spaces, dots, as well as parentheses, should not be used at the beginning of the name. There are also a set of reserved names that cannot be used as group names.

- For Group URL, used for the namespace, use only alphanumeric characters, dashes, dots, as well as underscores. However, the URL cannot start with dashes, or end with dots.

- Choose your visibility level. Public, Private, or Internal are the options offered.

- Personalize your experience with GitLab through answering questions like what your role is going to be, who will be able to use your group, what shall you be using this group for, etc.

- You will also have to invite fellow GitLab members as well as the other users to join this group.

Reserved Project and Group Names

All project and group names are not allowed, since they might conflict with the present routes that are being used by GitLab. There is a list of words that are not to be used as project or group names. They can be divided into three categories:

- **TOP_LEVEL_ROUTES:** These are names that have been reserved as user names or by top-level groups.

- **PROJECT_WILDCARD_ROUTES:** These are names that have been reserved for child groups as well as projects.

- **GROUP_ROUTES:** These are names which have been reserved for all groups and projects.

The project names you are not allowed to use currently are, \-, badges, blame, builds, blob, create, commits, edit, create_dir, files, environments/folders, gitlab-lfs/objects, find_file, info/lfs/objects, preview, new, refs, raw, update, tree, and wikis. Additionally, the reserved names for the groups include .well-known, \ -, 422.html, 404.html, 500.html, 502.html, 503.html, api, admin, apple-touch-icon-precomposed.png, apple-touch-icon.png, dashboard, assets, explore, deploy.html, favicon.png, favicon.ico, groups, files, help, health_check, import, help, jwt, login, profile, oauth, public, projects, robots.txt, search, s, sitemap, sitemap, sitemap.xml, sitemap.xml.gz, snippets, unsubscribes, uploads, users, v2, and slash-command-logo.png. Lastly, \- is unavailable as a subgroup name.

How to Create a Branch

A branch constitutes an independent line of development as far as a project is concerned. When you are creating a branch using your web interface or in your terminal window, you are essentially creating a snapshot of a particular branch, generally the main branch, in its present state. Then, as in Git, you are allowed to make changes in your feature branch, without affecting the main code line. The history of the changes made in your branch will be kept track of by the software. When you are done with making changes, you are allowed to merge them into the rest of the codebase using a merge request.

Feature Branch Workflow

Steps:

- Clone the project using the command -- git clone git@example.com:project-name.git.

- Create a branch of your feature

  ```
  git checkout -b $feature_name
  ```

- Write your code. Commit the changes with the command: git commit -am "My feature is ready".

- Push your branch to the GitLab: git push origin $feature_name.

- Review the code from the commits page.

- Carry out a merge request.

- Your team lead will now review the code, and then merge it to the main branch.

Creating Forks

A fork is a clone of an original repository that coders are supposed to put in another namespace where they can experiment as well as apply changes that might or might not be shared later, without affecting the main project. In order to create a fork on an existing project in GitLab:

- Go to the project's homepage, and click on the Fork option on the top right.

- Select the project you want to fork to. Below "Select a namespace to fork the project", make sure that you identify the project that you wish to fork to, and subsequently click on "Select". Only namespaces you have permissions for will be shown to you. Alternatively, if your GitLab administrator can manage to enable the experimental fork project form using the command "Feature.enable(:fork_project_form)", follow the instructions provided at the option "Creating a fork" providing your project name, URL, slug (i.e. path to a project), description (optional), as well as the visibility level you deem appropriate. However, bear in mind that the new fork project form is still under development and so, not ready for production use. It is found deployed behind a feature flag that is disabled by default, unless, as mentioned previously, GitLab administrators via the use of GitLab Rails Console can enable it.

GitLab creates your fork for you, and then redirects you to the project page for you to find it. The permissions that you have in the namespace will also be your permissions in the fork. If a public project with a repository feature set of the option "Members Only" is forked, the repository in the fork is public. The owner of that fork shall have to manually change its visibility.

Adding a File to a Repository

Adding files to a repository is a minor, but important task. Bringing different kinds of files to a repository, like code, documents, images, etc. will allow them to be tracked by Git's software, even if they have been created elsewhere.

You should be able to add a file to a repository in your terminal window, and then push the same to GitLab. You need to also be able to use the web interface, which might be a way simpler solution for you. If you want to create a file first, for example, a README.md text file, even that can be done from the terminal window or the web interface.

Create a New Issue

When you are able to create a new issue, you shall be prompted to fill in the data as well as the fields of the issue. If you happen to know the values that you want to assign to an issue, you should use the Quick Actions feature to be able to input the said values. When creating an issue, you should also associate it with an existing epic from a current group by selection using the Epic dropdown.

Creating Merge Requests

There are several ways you can employ in order to be able to create a merge request.

To create a merge request from a list of the merge-requests:

- From the top bar, select Menu>Projects, and subsequently find your project.

- On the left menu, choose Merge Requests.

- From the top right, select New Merge Request.

- Select a source as well as a target branch, followed by the option "Compare branches and continue".

- Fill out all fields and then click on Create merge request.

From an Issue

You can create a new branch from an issue, a feature introduced from GitLab 8.6 onward. If your development workflow ends up requiring an issue for every merge request that it has to make, you will have to create a branch directly from the issue in order to speed up the process. The new branch, and subsequently its merge request, will be marked as related to the issue at hand. After merging, the merge request will close the issue. You should be able to see a Create merge request dropdown below the location of the issue description. The Create merge request button will not be displayed in one of the following cases:

- A branch with the same name is already in existence.

- A merge request exists for this branch already.

- The project has an active fork relationship.

In order to make this button appear, try to remove the project's fork relationship. After you remove it, the fork relationship will not be able to be restored. The project will no longer be able to receive or send merge requests to the source projects, or the other forks. You will see a dropdown containing the options Create merge request and branch as well as Create branch. Select one of those options, a new branch or a branch, and your merge request will be created based on the default branch of your project. The name of a branch is based on an internal ID, as well as the issue title. If you will click on the Create branch button in an empty repository project, GitLab will be performing the following actions:

- Create a default branch.
- Commit a blank README.md file to it. It should Create as well as redirect you to a new branch based on the title of the issue.
- If your project was configured with a deployment service, like Kubernetes, GitLab will be prompting you to set up the option "auto deploy" by helping you create a file of the format .gitlab-ci.yml.

After the branch has been created, you should be able to edit files in the repository so that you can fix this issue. When you create a merge request based on the newly-created branch, the description field will display the issue closing pattern Closes #ID wherein "ID" is said to be the ID of the given issue. The issue will be closed after the merge request gets accepted.

When You Have to Add, Edit, or Upload a File
You can also create a merge request whenever you add, edit, or upload a file to a particular repository.

- Add, edit, or upload your file to the repository.
- Enter the reason for the commit made in the section "Commit Message".
- Select the Target branch or create a brand new branch by typing out your name (without using any capital letters, spaces, or special characters).

- Select the "Start a new merge request with these changes" checkbox or toggle. This checkbox or toggle needs to be visible only if the target happens to be different from the source branch, or if the source branch has been put under protection.

- Select "Commit Changes".

When You Create a Branch

To create merge requests on the creation of a branch:

- From the top bar, choose Menu>Projects to be able to find your project.

- In the left menu, select Repository>Branches.

- Type out a branch name and select the option "New Branch".

- On the right side above the file list, choose "Create Merge Request". A merge has been created. The default branch will be the target.

- Fill out all the blank fields, and choose "Create Merge Request".

When You Use Git Commands Locally

In order to create a merge request via running various Git commands on your local machine, follow the given steps:

- Create a branch using the command git checkout -b my-new-branch

- Create, edit, or delete the files as per your need. Then stage and commit them with the command:

```
git add.
git commit -m "My commit message"
```

- Push your branch to GitLab:

```
git push origin my-new-branch
```

GitLab will also prompt you to create a merge request using a direct link.

- Copy the same link and paste it in your browser.

You should also be able to add other flags to your commands when you are pushing through the command line in order to reduce the need for editing the merge requests manually via the use of UI.

When You Have to Work in a Fork

If you wish to create a merge request from your fork in order to be able to contribute to the main project, follow the given steps:

- From the top bar, select Menu>Project.

- Select your fork from the repository.

- From the left menu, go to the option "Merge Request", and select "New merge request".

- From the Source branch drop-down list box, select the branch from your forked repository as the source branch.

- Then, from the Target branch drop-down list box, select the branch of the upstream repository as a target branch. You should be able to set a default target project in order to change the default target branch, a useful method if you are working on a forked project.

- Select Compare branches and continue.

- Click on Submit merge request.

After your work has been merged, if you do not intend to make any further contributions to your upstream project, then you should ideally unlink your fork from it. For this purpose, go to Settings>Advanced Settings, and eliminate the forking relationship.

By Sending an Email

A brief caveat: the standard format of the generated email address was changed from GitLab 11.7 onward. The earlier format is still being supported so the existing aliases as well as contacts will still be able to work. Now, coming to the main point, you should be able to create a merge request by sending out an email to GitLab. The merge request-target branch is always the project's default branch.

What needs to be ensured:

- A GitLab administrator will have to configure the incoming mail.

- A GitLab administrator will have to configure the Reply by email.

In order to create a merge request by sending out an email

- From the top bar, select Menu>Projects in order to be able to find your project.

- Go to the top left menu, select the option "Merge Requests".

- From the top right, select the option "Email a new merge request to this project". An email address will be displayed. You must copy this address, and also make sure that it stays private.

- Open an email and compose a message containing the following information: the TO line must be the email address that you copied, the subject line has to be the source branch name, and the message body has got to be the merge request description.

- Send the email.

Your merge request shall be created.

Add Attachments When Creating Merge Request by Email
From GitLab 11.5 onward, you are allowed to add commits to a merge request simply by adding patches as attachments to your email. All attachments with a filename that ends with .patch are considered as patches, and processed ordered by name. The combined size of all the patches can be upto 2 MB. If the source branch from the subject is non-existent, it can be created from the repository's HEAD or the specified target branch. You should also be able to specify the target branch by using the command/target_branch

quick action. If the source branch is already in existence, the patches are usually applied on the top of it.

Set the Default Target Project

The source and the target project of merge requests are usually the same, unless some forking has been involved. Creating a fork of the project could cause one of the two scenarios, especially if you are creating a new merge request:

- You will target an upstream project, i.e. the project you forked as well as the default option.

- You will target your own fork.

In order to have merge requests from a fork by default target your own fork (rather than the upstream project), you will need to change the default.

- On the top bar, choose Menu>Project.

- From the left side of the menu, click on "Settings", then "General", then "Merge Requests".

- In the Target project section, choose the option which you want to use for the default target project.

- Click on "Save Changes".

Working with Projects

Most of the work in GitLab consists of a project. Files and codes are to be saved in projects, and most of the features tend to be within the scope of projects. For you to be able to explore the most popular projects available on GitLab, follow the given steps:

- From the top bar, select Menu>Project.
- Click on Explore Projects.

GitLab tends to display a list of projects, sorted according to the last updated date. To view the projects with the most stars, click on Most stars. To be able to view projects with the most number of comments in the past month, click on Trending. Do keep in mind that by default, /explore is visible to unauthorized users as well. But, if the public visibility level has been restricted, /explore should be visible only to signed-in users.

In order to create a new blank project on the New Project page:

- Click on "Create Blank Project."

- Provide the mentioned information: first, the name of the project in the field "Project name". Bear in mind that you are not allowed to use special characters, but you can use hyphens, spaces, underscores, and even emojis. When adding the name, the Project slug tends to auto-populate. The slug is what the GitLab instance will be using as the URL, i.e. the path to the project. If you want a different slug, you will have to input the project name first, and then change the slug later.

    Second, the path of your project in the Project slug field. This is the URL path of your project that GitLab instance tends to use. If you left the space for the Project name as blank, it will auto-populate anyway when you fill in the space for Project slug.

The project description (is optional) will allow you to provide a description for your project's dashboard, which should help others in understanding what your project primarily is about. As mentioned previously, it is not necessarily required. Nevertheless, it is a good idea to fill this section in anyway.

Ensure that you change the visibility level as per your project's access as well as viewing rights for its users.

Select "Initialize Repository with a README" option in order to create a README file, so that when your Git Repository is initialized, it has a default branch, and also can be cloned.

- Finally, click on "Create Project."

Project Templates

Project Templates are important since they are able to pre-populate a new project with all the necessary files that you shall need to get started quickly. There are two different kinds of project templates:

- Built-in Templates that tend to be sourced, developed and maintained from project templates as well as other page groups.

- Custom Project Templates, for custom templates that have been configured by GitLab administrators as well as users. To be able to use a built template on the

New Project page: first, click on Click from template. Select the Built-in tab. From the available list of templates, click on the preview button, to see the template source itself, as well as the Use template button, in order to start creating a project. Lastly, finish creating the project by filling out the details of the project. This process is the same as creating a blank project.

Enterprise Templates

GitLab is also developing Enterprise templates in order to help you streamline your audit management with a few selected regulatory standards. These templates should be able to automatically import the issues that will correspond to each regulatory requirement. To create a new project with an Enterprise template, follow these steps on the New project page:

- Click on "Create from template."

- Press the button that shall take you to the built-in tab.

- There should be a list of built-in Enterprise templates that are available. Press on the Preview button to look at the source of the template. Then, use the "Use Template" button so that you can start creating your project.

- Finish the task at hand by filling out the details of the project. This process tends to be the same as that of creating a blank project.

GitLab can also furnish the HIPAA Audit Protocol Template, which was first provided in GitLab 12.10. Further, GitLab also provides you with the space as well as the avenues to improve upon the existing built-in templates or even contribute new ones that you yourself have developed.

Custom Project Templates

These were introduced in GitLab 11.2. Being able to create new projects based on the custom templates for projects is a highly convenient option to ensure that you are quickly able to start your projects. Custom projects are available from the Instance (at instance level), as well as at the group level from the Group tab in the Create from template page. In order to be able to create a custom project template on the New Project page:

- Click on "Create from template".

- Select either the Instance tab or the Group tab.

- There will be a list of the available custom templates. You could click on the Preview button to see the template source, and the Use Template button in order to be able to start creating your projects.

- Lastly, finish creating your project by filling out its details. Here also, the process tends to be the same as creating a blank project.

Next, we will learn about how to push to create a new project. This feature was introduced from GitLab Version 10.5. Basically, when you have created a new repository locally, you do not have to sign in to the GitLab interface in order to create a project as well as clone its repository. You should be able to directly push your new repository to the GitLab, which should be able to create your new project without leaving your terminal. In order to push for a new project, follow the given steps:

- Identify the namespace to which you want to add the new project, as you will be needing this information in order to carry out a future step. To be able to determine if you have permission to create new projects in a particular namespace, view the page of the group in a web browser to ascertain that the page displays a New project button. Since project creation permissions are dependent on a multitude of factors, you will be well advised to reach out to your GitLab administrator if you are unsure.

- If you wish to push during SSH, make sure that you have created an SSH key and also added it to your GitLab account.

- You can push using various methods. Here, do make sure that you give the domain name of the machine hosting your Git repository instead of gitlab.example.com, the name of your namespace instead of "namespace", as well as the name of your new project, instead of "myproject". To push with SSH, the required command will be git push --set-upstream git@gitlab.example.com:namespace/myproject.git master. On the other hand, to make the push with HTTPS: git push --set-upstream https://gitlab.example.com/namespace/myproject.git.master. Additionally, in order to export your existing repository tags, you will be well advised to append the --tags flag to your git push command.

- When the push is completed, a message from GitLab will let you know that your project was created.

- To configure the remote, you will have to alter the command git remote add origin https://gitlab.example.com/namespace/myproject.git in order to provide your namespace as well as project names. However, this step is optional and so completely up to you.

You should now be able to see your new project at https://gitlab.example.com/namespace/myproject. Your project's visibility is always Private by default, but you can always go and change it from your project's settings. There is a prerequisite though, you must have the role of an owner for the particular group whose visibility you want to change. The steps to do so are following:

- From the top bar, select Menu>Groups and then find your project.

- From the left sidebar, select Settings>General.

- Expand the options Naming as well as Visibility.

- For the visibility level, choose Private, Internal, or Public.

- Click on Save Changes.

Star a Project

Starring a project will make it easier for you to find it among other projects that you frequently use as well. The number of stars a project is associated with also indicates its popularity. In order to star a project:

- Go to the homepage of the project that you wish to star.
- Click on the option of "Star" that you will find in the upper right corner of the page.

In order to view your starred projects:

- Select the options Menu>Project from the top bar.
- Click on "Starred Projects".
- GitLab will display a range of information regarding your starred projects, including: project description (i.e. name, description, as well as icon), number of times that the project has been starred, number of forks the project contains, number of open issues as well as merge requests, etc.

To delete a project, navigate through the home page of that project, and follow the provided steps:

- Go to Settings>General.
- Expand upon the Advanced section.
- Scroll down to the delete project section.
- Click on Delete project.
- Confirm the action by typing out the expected text.

Projects that are located in the personal namespaces shall be deleted immediately on request.

Apart from that, you can also enable delayed project removal, by configuring your projects in a group (but not your personal namespace) to get deleted later, i.e. after a delayed interval, during which the projects are in a read-only state and can still be restored. The default interval period is seven days, but it can also be configured. You can also change the period to 0, thus enabling the immediate removal of projects as well as groups. This feature of default deletion delay has been introduced from GitLab 12.6. The steps are fairly simple:

- Select the desired option.

- Click on Save Changes.

On GitLab.com, you would have to find the settings page in order to find out what the default setting is. To allow for delayed deletion of projects in a particular group, follow the given steps:

- Go to Settings>General.

- Make sure that you expand the Permissions, LFS, as well as 2FA section.

- Check the option "Enable Delayed Project Removal".

- This is optional. In order to prevent the subgroups from being able to change the settings, select the option "Enforce for all subgroups".

- Click on "Save Changes".

Note: From GitLab 13.11 and onward, the group setting for delayed project removal is inherited by subgroups. However, as per the rules of the Cascading settings, these inheritances can be overruled, unless they have been enforced by an ancestor.

You can also prevent the forking of projects outside the group. This feature was introduced from GitLab 13.3 and onward. As we all know by now, by default, the projects of a group can be forked. On the Premium and higher tiers, you can stop the projects in a group from getting forked outside of the present top-tier group. Earlier, this setting was available only for the groups that enforced a Group Managed Account in Security Assertion Markup Language (SAML). This setting can also be removed from the SAML setting page, and subsequently migrated to the page meant for group settings. In the interim, both of these settings are to be taken into consideration. Even if one of them happens to be true, the group will not be able to allow outside forks. Here is the list of steps you need to follow to prevent your projects from being forked outside the group:

- Choose Settings>General from the page of the top-level group.

- Expand the sections meant for Permissions, 2FA, as well as LFS.

- Check the option "Prevent project forking outside current group".

- Press on "Save Changes".

Do not worry. The existing forks shall not be removed.

Group Push Rules

Group Push Rules allows for the maintainers of a group to establish push rules for the new projects of a specific group. To configure the push rules for a group, you shall have to follow the provided set of instructions:

- Go to that particular group's Push Rules page.

- Select the settings that you desire.

- Select the option "Save Push Rules".

The new subgroups of a group will have push rules decided for them based on these factors:

- The closest parent group with its push rules defined.

- Push rules that have been set at an instance level, if the push rules of the parent groups have not been defined.

Checking If Access Was Blocked Due to IP Restriction

If a user comes across a 404 message when s/he was expecting regular access, and the problem seems to be limited to a particular group, search for auth.log rails log for the given:

- **json.message:** "Attempting to access IP restricted Group"

- **json.allowed:** false

When you are viewing these log entries, compare your remote.ip with the list of permitted IPs for the group.

These are some of the GitLab basics whose functionality you need to be well versed with in order to operate Git on it. Nevertheless, this guide is by no means exhaustive, and you should be able to understand the workings of the software as you use it in practical settings.

FREE AND ENTERPRISE ACCOUNTS

Now, let's briefly move to the pricing plan offered by GitLab.

- **FREE:** This plan will provide free-forever features to individual users. Needless to say, it is absolutely free of cost. The features you will be provided with include the span of a DevOps lifecycle, free static websites, 400 CI/CD minutes per month.

- **PREMIUM:** This pack will enhance team productivity as well as coordination. It is priced at $19 per user per month, amounting to the annual bill of 228 USD (the prices mentioned are usually subject to the applicable local as well as withholding taxes, they will probably also vary if you do not purchase them directly via the company, but through a partner or a reseller). The features provided will be everything that is present in the Free pack, along with other features like advanced CI/CD, faster code reviews, release controls, agile Enterprise planning, Self-managed reliability, as well as 10,000 CI/CD minutes per month.

- **ULTIMATE:** This is an Enterprise Account. This pack will ensure that you acquire organization-wide security, compliance, as well as planning. It costs $99 per user per month, and billed annually at 1188 USD.

The features provided include everything from the Premium pack as well as native cloud security, advanced security testing, portfolio management, ensuring compliance, value stream management, allowing free guest users, as well as providing upto 50,000 CI/CD minutes per month.

All the plans provide unlimited private repositories. They can be used as SaaS or Self-Managed. But what are SaaS and self-managed? GitLab can also be divided into GitLab SaaS and GitLab Self-Managed. In the case of the former, the company will host the project, and you would not have to worry about downloading and installing the GitLab software yourself. Additionally, no technical setup is required. For GitLab Self-Managed on the other hand, you will play the part of the host. This software shall require the Linux experience. You will have to download and install the software on your own infrastructure, or you could do so in the public cloud environment offered by the company.

In this chapter, we delved into GitLab, what it exactly is, the history of its development and acquisitions, several elements of its functionality, different kinds of accounts available, etc. Moving to the next chapter, we shall be dealing with BitBucket, looking at it through a similar lens, with an emphasis on its definition and functions as well as its history and the various types of accounts that are available on it. So, read on.

CHAPTER 8

Bitbucket

IN THIS CHAPTER

➢ What is Bitbucket

➢ History of Bitbucket

➢ How to use Bitbucket

➢ Free and Enterprise accounts

In the previous chapter, we learned about GitLab, what it is, its history, functionality, and commands, the accounts it offers, etc. Now, we move on to Bitbucket, with a similar set of concerns in mind. So, let us proceed.

WHAT IS BITBUCKET

Bitbucket is a Git-based source code repository hosting service that happens to be owned by Atlassian Corporation Plc. (Programmable Logic Controller), an Australian software company which develops products for project managers,

DOI: 10.1201/9781003229100-8

software developers, as well as other software development teams. Atlassian acquired Bitbucket in 2010. Bitbucket was then recognized as a hosted service that was used to enable code collaboration. In May 2012, Atlassian released Stash, a Git repository that was meant for enterprises, and rechristened it as Bitbucket Server. Bitbucket offers free accounts as well as commercial plans with unlimited private repositories. It provides collaborative version control, and is available in a plethora of languages like English, Russian, German, Chinese, French, Spanish, Japanese, Hindi, Korean, as well as Portuguese. The official URL is BitBucket.org, while the name of the creator is Jesper Noehr. The service registration requires an optional OpenID, which is a decentralized as well as open standard authentication protocol that was promoted by the non-profit organization OpenID Foundation. The service is presently available online, and was launched 13 years ago in 2008 using Python, a high-level interpreted general-purpose programming language.

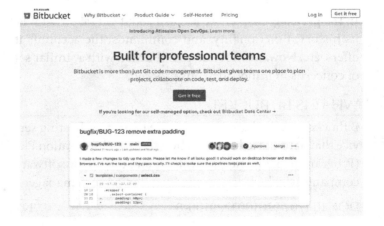

Services

Bitbucket Cloud

Bitbucket Cloud (earlier known as just Bitbucket) is written in Python and utilizes Django, a web framework following the model-template-views, i.e. the MTV architectural pattern. Mostly, Bitbucket is only used for code as well as code reviews. The service provides a plethora of features like:

- Bitbucket pipelines, a regular as well as continuous delivery service.

- Pull requests with code reviews along with comments.

- Two-Step Verification.

- IP Whitelisting.

- Merge Checks.

- Code Search (Alpha).

- Git Large File Storage (LFS).

- Issue-tracking.

- Wikis.

- Documentation, including automatically rendered README files from a plethora of Markdown-like file formats. Markdown here is a lightweight markup language which can be used for adding formatting elements to plaintext format text documents.

- Static sites that are being hosted on Bitbucket Cloud, i.e. the static websites having the Bitbucket.io domain in their URL.

- Add-ons as well as integrations.

- Snippets that allow the developers to share code segments as well as files.

- Smart Mirroring.

- Representational State Transfer (REST) Application Programming Interface (APIs) that allow you to build various third-party applications which should be able to use any kind of development language. A REST API is an application programming interface that conforms to the constraints of REST Architectural style as well as allows for interaction with the RESTful Web Services. REST was invented and developed by the computer scientist Roy Fielding.

So, Bitbucket is our Git repository management solution that is designed for highly professional teams. It will give you a central place so that you are able to manage all your Git repositories, collaborate with your fellow developers for your source code, as well as guide you through the development flow. It gives you amazing facilities like:

- Access Control so that you are able to restrict access to your source code.

- Workflow control in order to be able to enforce a project or a team workflow.

- Jira Integration that provides full development traceability.

- Full Rest API in order to be able to build features that are customized to your specific workflow.

Now, let's discuss how to go about operating on Bitbucket using instructions for a variety of functions like:

Granting Repository Access to Users and Groups

Whenever you create a repository, you have got to specify whether it is supposed to be public or private. If your repository is public, anyone should be able to access it. However, if it is private, only a few selected list of individuals as well as groups will have access to it.

To create groups, you shall have to go to the User Groups page of your workspace Settings. If you happened to have created a new group for a workspace, Bitbucket would not automatically add it to the existing repositories of the workspace. Alternatively, if you create a new group from the designated workspace, Bitbucket will not be adding it to the list of your personal repositories. Users, as well as groups, usually have one of the provided levels of access:

- **Admin:** This level will allow the users to do everything within a particular repository, like change the settings of the repository, update the user permissions, as well as delete the entire repository.

- **Write:** This will allow the users to contribute to the repository by being able to push the changes directly.

- **Read:** This will allow the users to view, clone, as well as fork the repository code, but not push the changes. Read Access will also allow the users to be able to create issues, comment on the said issues, edit wiki pages, etc.

Steps:

- **User Access:** Make sure that you enter a user as well as an access type to be able to add a user to a repo.

- **Group Access:** Pick a group and then access type to add a group to a particular repo.

- **Remove:** Click to be able to remove access for a user or a group.

- **Change Access:** Click on any of the access types to change the access for a user or a group.

If a user happens to delete his or her account, Bitbucket will be automatically deleting that particular user from all their repository access lists.

For when you are adding users, remember that if you are on a free plan and the number of users who happen to have access to your private repositories is going over five, the access will be becoming read-only until you manage to upgrade your account or at least remove users from a group or the individual repositories. You along with the other repository administrators will still be having access to the repository. Also, you will not be able to add a workspace to your repository. The only workspace that has access will have to be the workspace that owns the repository, but you should also be able to transfer repositories to your workspace if you deem it necessary. Or else, create a new group and subsequently, add the specific users that you want to that particular group.

You must also learn how to add group access to a repository. Whenever you create a new repository, Bitbucket checks to see if the owner of the repository is in any groups with an access level of read, write, or admin. If the workspace does, Bitbucket will be adding those groups to the new repository alongside a default permission. If a group does not have any access, that group shall not be appearing on the "User and group access" page. However, you should still be able to add that group along with all the required as well as suitable access. These are the steps to follow:

- Go to the User and Group Access page, click on the option "Select a group" and subsequently scroll down to your new group or start typing its name in the text box to be able to find it.

- After you have made the selection of the right group, select the suitable access level from your access dropdown list.

- Click on "Add" and add the group to the repository.

Update User/Group Access

In order to be able to update group access, click the new access level of the group from the page "User and Group Access". When you are done with changing your group access or removing a group from the repository entirely, you will be able to establish repository-level group settings. These changes shall remain in effect for that specific repository, even if you were to later change the group's access from the workspace or the account's User group's page.

While user groups are generally the best way to manage access to your repositories, you should also be able to add the users individually. In order to be able to add individual users to your repository:

- Go to the User and Group Access page, enter the name as well as the email address of a user of Bitbucket inside the Users text box.

- Choose an access level from the options available in the dropdown menu.

- Press the button "Add".

If you are adding the email address of someone without their account, that person shall be receiving an email prompting them to create one. Once the user has access to Bitbucket, s/he will be able to access the repository as well.

Branch Permissions

For Bitbucket, branch permissions should help you to enforce specific workflows as well as prevent errors like a workspace member managing to delete the master branch. With proper branch permissions, you should be able to:

- Closely control the users as well as the groups who are allowed to write or merge to any branch.

- Create permissions for a particular branch type, as well as pattern. For example, ensure that/Project limits its access to all branches that have names like Project 1/2/3, and so on.

If you need even tighter control over the workflow of your workspace, you should check out the feature of merge checks.

They will allow you to recommend or even require particular conditions on your merges for individual branches as well as the branch patterns. We will also be looking at the different aspects of merge checks in the next section of this chapter. If you have got the branching model enabled, you should be able to configure permissions for all the branches of a particular type. This can prove to be exceptionally useful when you wish to restrict the merge access on all the release branches, for example. Not only that, the software of Bitbucket makes sure that the branch permissions are never overlapping with each other.

Suggesting or Requiring Checks before a Merge Takes Place

Merge checks are defined as checks that allow you to recommend as well as require the particular conditions on merges for the branch patterns as well as the individual branches. Merge checks are supposed to be working in tandem with the branch permissions in order to give the members of the workspace some flexibility as well as control over their development workflow. Providing the users with these recommended checks for their consideration before they conduct the merge is available to everyone on Bitbucket. Nevertheless, there are also options available to conduct the Premium Merge Checks:

- Enforce the merge checks to ensure that every pull request is completely vetted before the actual act of merge takes place.

- Ask for another approval from the reviewers, if the source branch of a pull request happens to get modified.

There are different purposes that merge checks tend to serve. They are:

- Dependent Merges
  - These will ensure that users are only able to merge changes with the passing builds.
  - Select a particular number of successful builds before actually conducting the merge.
  - Can be used with Bitbucket Pipelines, a build tool integration or the commit status REST API.

- Code Review Completion
  - It ties your merges to the code reviews.
  - Allows your colleagues to work collaboratively with the aid of pull requests at their disposal.
  - Keep your workflow consistent so that the developers always know what they need to do in order to conduct the merge.

- Task Completion
  - You will be able to create tasks on pull requests in order to mark out the changes that have to be made.
  - Management of a pull request as it is progressing toward approval.
  - Make sure that all the tasks in a pull request are completed before the final merge is conducted.

To reiterate, you will need to use merge checks for purposes of recommendation as well as requiring that a set of conditions be met before a merge gets actually conducted. If you select any of the options that have been provided below, but you do not have the Premium plan, Atlassian will warn the users that they still have unresolved merge checks, but will not stop the act of merging if the user still wishes to proceed. If you want your users or developers to be prevented from merging, you will need to upgrade to a Premium plan and further select "Prevent a merge with unresolved merge checks". Some of the important merge checks are:

Setting	Result
Check for at least {#number} approvals	Users will get a notification if/when their pull requests do not have the prescribed number of approvals.
Check for the unresolved pull request tasks	Users should get a notification whenever they have pull request tasks that are yet to be finished.
Check for {#} passed builds in the last commit	Users shall get a notification if and when they do not have the prescribed number of successful builds in their most recent commit.
Automatically merge a pull request when all the checks are passed	The admin should enable this feature so that so that a queued up merge will be triggered automatically once all the merge checks have been successfully passed.

Furthermore, on the Premium plan, you shall also have access to the given settings:

Setting	Result
Enforce all the merge checks to ensure that every pull request has been completely vetted before the merge takes place	Here, users will not be able to conduct the merge as long as their pull requests continue to have unresolved merge checks. They will get to see a checklist of all the issues that they need to resolve via their codes before it might be allowed for the merge to be executed.
Reset the approvals when your source branch has been modified	If any changes are made to the source branch of the pull request, the pull request will be making automatic updates without seeking any kind of approval, and the reviewers shall subsequently have to review as well as approve of the pull request again.

You need to first navigate to the repository where you wish to add the branch permissions, then follow it up by going to Repository Settings>Branch permissions. In order to add permissions as well as merge checks to the main branch, take care to follow the given set of instructions:

- Click on "Add a branch permission".

- Enter the provided details into each field: Branch (in this case, Main), Write Access (the individual you want to automatically get the merge through the pull request permissions), and Merge via pull request (again, the name of the said individual).

- Expand "Add merge checks", then click on "Checked for {#} passed builds on the last commit", and add a number from the dropdown options.

- Click on Save.

This setup should help the member of your workspace have access control to the central branch. Because only the production-ready code has to be merged, a merge check is required only for the successful builds.

Next, how to add permissions as well as merge checks to a developing branch:

- Click on "Add a branch permission".

- You, then need to enter the following details into each of the fields that have been mentioned here: the name of the branch or the pattern, write access, as well as who gets to Merge via the pull requests.

- Expand the Add Merge Checks: Click on "Check for at least {#} approvals" and select the suitable number from the list of dropdown options, subsequently, click on "Check for at least {#} approval from default reviewers" and choose the number of default reviewers that you want, if you have established any for this pull request, from whom you want to approve the pull request, then click on "Check for the unresolved pull request tasks", for the option "Check for {#} passed builds on the last commit" choose the number you want from the dropdown options.

- Finally, click on Save.

Using Pull Requests for Code Review

After you have added files as well as made updates in the existing code, it is time to merge that code into your Bitbucket Cloud Repository. Before you make the merge, you will have to ensure that the quality of the code is consistent with, and will not harm, break, or tamper with any of the existing, tried and tested features in the code. To be able to receive the feedback that your code needs for you to undertake improvements as well as updates, you should create a pull request that must include all the lines of code that you have contributed to the project. Pull Requests importantly provide you with a method for requesting reviews for your code from your colleagues as well as checking the build status dependent on your latest commit made. As far as the larger workflow is concerned, to use pull requests, you require a branch or a fork, so that you are able to develop your code on a separate line from the primary codebase.

Pull Request Process

Collaboration as well as code review are the core of pull requests. Depending on your role in the process of code development, whether you are an author or a reviewer, or both, you are supposed to make use of the pull requests.

Pull Request Authors

If you are searching for and want to find out the pull requests that you created, you will have to check for the option "Your pull requests" list on the "Your Work" option on your dashboard. As a pull request author, it is imperative that the code review process begins after you have created and sent a pull request to your reviewers. If you could not add the viewers during the creation, you can always go back to the pull request and edit it to add them later on. After you have created the pull request as well as added the reviewers, you should ideally wait to receive their approvals. However, the iterations and the deliberations will soon begin as the reviewers will start looking through your code as well as making comments. You will also be receiving the email notifications of the ongoing discussions, where you must participate, keeping your point across with clarity as well as precision, thus becoming an active contributor in the code review process.

Pull Request Reviewers

To find out the requests that you have been asked to review, check for the "Pull Requests to Review" list on the "Your Work" dashboard. You also could go to the Pull Requests page in the repositories of your workspace if you wish to help your colleagues with the other pull requests that they are supposed to check. Whenever a workspace member will add you as a reviewer, Bitbucket shall notify you over email. Post the initial notification regarding the pull request creation, you will keep on getting email notifications with regard to the following actions:

- The author has made updates.

- Another user has made a comment.

- A reviewer has sent approval.

- The user has merged the pull request.

If you seek to disable these notifications, you shall have to unwatch the pull request. During the code review, you will have to comment with your suggestions, feedback, as well as ideas. You must take your time to consider if there are logic errors, if all the cases have been fully implemented, if there are existing automated tests that need to be rewritten, as well as whether the code conforms to the existing style guidelines. After you are done with your review, if you deem the pull request to be ready for merging (or if you trust that the author shall be able to resolve the issues pointed out before merge), you should click on the Approve button at the top right. A green checkmark would appear next to your name in the Reviewers section after you send an approval for a pull request. Do remember that if your workspace operates on a Premium plan, the admins might not be able to pull requests that do not contain a certain number of approvals from being merged.

How to Restore a Deleted Branch

Sometimes, it is possible for you to accidentally delete an entire branch. For cases like these, make sure everything is being performed locally, as well as that your repo is in the state that you need it to be in, before making a push to the Bitbucket Cloud. It will again be a good idea for you to clone your repo, and then perform these solutions first.

- If you deleted a branch, you should be able to see something similar on your terminal window:

```
Deleted branch <branch-name> (was <sha>)
```

- If you need to restore the branch, you will have to make use of the command:

```
git checkout -b <branch> <sha>
```

Say, you don't remember the SHA, then you could,

- Find the SHA for the commit at the tip of the branch you deleted using the git reflog command.

- Now, to restore the branch, use 'git checkout -b <branch> <sha>.

Say, if the commits are not there in your reflog,

- You should try recovering the branch by resetting it to the SHA of the commit found.

- You should then be able to display every commit using either of these:

```
git log -p<commit>
git cat-file -p <commit>
```

Bitbucket Server

Bitbucket Server (earlier known as Stash) is a combination of web interface product as well as a Git server that is written in Java, a class-based, high-level, object-oriented programming language designed so that it has as less implementation dependencies as possible, and built with Apache Maven, a built-automation tool that is mostly used for Java projects. Bitbucket Server allows its users to be able to do basic Git operations (like merging code or reviewing, similar to GitHub) while also being able to control the read as well as the write access to code. It also allows for integration with other products of Atlassian. Bitbucket Server is also a commercial software product that can be licensed for running on-premises. Atlassian provides Bitbucket Servers to open source projects meeting a specified criteria for free, as well as to the non-profit organizations and other organizations that happen to be non-academic, non-government, non-political, non-commercial, and secular. For commercial as well as academic consumers, the complete source code is available, albeit under a developer source license.

HISTORY

Bitbucket, earlier, was an independent startup company that was founded by Jesper Nøhr in 2008. On September 29, 2010, Bitbucket got acquired by Atlassian. Bitbucket was then popularly known as a Mercurial Project Hosting site. Mercurial, referenced earlier in this book, is a distributed revision control tool meant to be used by software developers that was released in 2005. The product development and software company Atlassian had already made it clear that it would be investing heavily in the enterprise space. Neither of the parties ended up disclosing the terms and conditions of the deal. Bitbucket then used to play host to over 60,000 accounts and was the premier code collaboration provider for the distributed VCS offered by Mercurial as well as a general services provider for the developers who wished to share as well as encourage collaboration in their projects. Bitbucket was understood as being quite similar to GitHub as well as Google Code, and was also hosting the codes of many incredible open-source projects like Adium, Opera, MailChimp, etc. Bitbucket was incorporated into Atlassian's family of an extensive range of development products and software collaboration tools that were helping various teams to conceive, plan, develop, as well as launch their products. These products had included the issue tracker JIRA as well as Confluence (known to be a facilitator of content collaboration). The company's offerings, even then, were utilized by more than 20,000 customers worldwide, including organizations like Zynga, Cisco, Adobe, as well as Facebook. As per the decisions made during the process of integration, Atlassian made Bitbucket completely and absolutely free, apart from offering free hosting for as many as 5-devs, and giving out unlimited repositories as well. At the time of the launch of Bitbucket as an Atlassian product, the company also offered a free year for a ten-user account, as a promotional tactic. The company representatives had been quoted saying that the acquisition had helped the company in filling a lacuna in its product offerings, and had thus made Atlassian a significantly more comprehensive platform for its customers involved in the field of software development. The developers had finally got a place to host their code, as well as keep a track of their project issues within the domain of Atlassian. The company's Jay Simon had then declared that the company was seeking to become what Adobe was for designers, except for the technical development teams. By September 2015, Atlassian renamed their Stash product as Bitbucket Server. In July 2016, Bitbucket was added as support for Git LFS. Then in 2020, Bitbucket removed its support for its original repository, the format of Mercurial, a distributed revision control tool that is meant to be used by software developers for their projects, and is supported on Microsoft Windows, as well as Unix-like operating systems of FreeBSD (Berkeley Distribution Software), macOS, as well as Linux.

FREE AND ENTERPRISE ACCOUNTS

This section is a guide on how to manage your plan as well as billing for the Bitbucket Cloud. Basically, Bitbucket Cloud provides an unlimited number of private as well as public repositories to everyone who has a free account. You are allowed to grant as many users as you want to be able to have access to your public repositories. Bitbucket will also determine the cost depending on the number of users who will be able to have access to your private repositories. There are three different plans provided by the company: they are called free, standard, as well as premium. Each plan is accompanied by a given amount of build minutes for Pipelines, as well as a mandated file storage for Git LFS, but you should also be able to acquire additional storage as well as minutes. Keep in mind that updating your current plan will not be able to increase the size of your repository. There is a given size limit for the repositories—2 GB. This applies to all plans, Free, Standard, as well as Premium.

Let's briefly delve into the features provided by each plan.

Free

- It is free of cost for upto five users.

- It provides 50 build minutes per month and has the LFS of 1 GB in all.

- It does not provide Overage protection.

Standard

- It costs $3 every user per month, or a flat rate of $15 per month for any number of users from one to five.

- The build minutes are 2500 per minute per month, while the LFS is 5 GB in all.

- It provides overage protection.

Premium

- It costs $6 per user per month, or a flat rate of $30 per month for any number of users ranging between one and five.

- The total build minutes provided are 3500 per minute per month, and the LFS is 10 GB in all. Other features provided include deployment permissions, IP allowlisting, merge checks, requiring 2SV, access controls, etc.

- Overage protection is included.

However, keep in mind that these plans and prices go through a regular process of changes as well as revisions, so you should check the official page of Bitbucket for perfectly updated plans as well as prices.

Overage Protection

The standard as well as the premium plans includes overage protection for your build minutes as well as a LFS for all users belonging to the workspace. However, if you happen to go over your build minutes, Bitbucket will automatically add more minutes in your current month. But when the next billing cycle starts, the build minute usage will reset, and you will not be billed the additional charge (unless you have gone over the limit again). Similarly, if you go beyond the limit of the LFS, Bitbucket will again automatically add more to the LFS capacity. You shall continue to be billed for the supplementary LFS capacity on a monthly basis cost per 100 GB of additional storage as long as you will be using it. The charges of overages are $10 per 1000 additional build minutes for each billing cycle, as well as the same price, i.e. $10 per 100 GB of LFS, as per your needs.

If you happen to be on the free plan, make sure that you are able to purchase additional storage or minutes, whatever it is that you require in order to be able to complete your work. You shall have to enter the details required of a credit card that is associated with your Bitbucket account. Rest assured, you will be billed if and only if you have exceeded the limit that had been explicitly mentioned in your plan, whether it will be for storage or the build minutes. However, if you choose to not purchase any additional minutes or storage, and still end up going over the prescribed limit, you shall not be able to run more pipelines in that particular month or even use more LFS.

Changing Your Plan

In order to change your current Bitbucket plan, follow the provided steps:

- Open your Workspace settings via clicking on "Your profile and settings" avatar> the name of the current workspace, and subsequently click on "Settings" from the left sidebar.

- Choose Plan details under Plans and Billing on the left panel.

- Click on "Upgrade plan" or "Change plan".

- On the Bitbucket Cloud plans page, click on one among the Free, Standard, or Premium buttons for the plan that you need.

- In the section for "Enter your billing details", enter the required information.

- Click on Purchase.

In the case of the free plan with extra minutes as well as storage, under the section "Free plan", depending on your plan, you will see the options "Get more minutes and storage" or "Only pay for extra storage and minutes". Click on these options, if you need extra minutes as well as storage along with the Free plan. If you are paying for extra storage as well as minutes alongside the Free plan and now wish to stop, you will be able to see an option "Stop paying for storage and minutes".

Once you are done, your payment information is recorded and now, you should be able to see your new plan in the Plan Details page. Your credit card will be billed monthly as per the plan that you have chosen as well as the number of users on your account. If you happen to miss a payment, you get downgraded to a Free plan with a five-user limit. If you used to have the premium plan, you will now lose any saved Premium settings.

Updated Credit Card Details
If you wish to change a credit card that has been associated with your account, do take care to follow all the mentioned steps:

- Open the Workspace settings by clicking on Your profile and settings avatar>the name of the workspace, and subsequently click on settings in the left sidebar.

- Select the option "Plan Details" under Plans and Billing on the left panel. You should be able to see your credit card details in the section for the Billing details at the right side of your plan details.

- Click on the option "Update Credit Card". If you have not been able to add your credit card yet, you will also have to use another option that you will clearly be able to see called "Add credit card".

- On the "Enter your billing Details" screen, make the appropriate changes as per your needs to your credit card details.

- Lastly, click on the "Purchase" option.

Remember that whenever you have to make updates to anything on this screen, you shall have to re-enter your credit card information.

See the Users on Your Plan

If you wish to see the users that are currently on your Bitbucket plan, you will have to follow the provided steps:

- Open your Workspace settings by clicking on "Your profile and settings">the name of the workspace, and then subsequently click on settings in the left sidebar.

- On the left panel, select the option "Users on Plan" under Plans and Billing.

- On the Users on Plan page, you shall be able to see all the users who have access to your private repositories. From there, click on "View Access" to be able to see which repositories they have access to as well as the groups that they are a part of. Click on the icon of "X" to remove the users from this list, which should also be able to remove them from those repositories as well as groups.

Additionally, there are three deployment options that are available, as far as the case of Bitbucket is concerned. They are:

- **Bitbucket Cloud:** It is hosted on Atlassian's servers and accessed through the use of a URL. Bitbucket Cloud provides its users with Pipelines, an exclusive as well as a built-in continuous integration tool, enabling you to build, test, as well as deploy from directly within your Bitbucket. However, there are also some restricted functions in the Atlassian Cloud Apps.

- **Bitbucket Server:** It is hosted on-location and within your environment. Bitbucket Server will not come with a built-in testing or deployment tool, but it does tend to have a strong system of integration with Bamboo, the popular continuous integration as well as continuous delivery tool that should be able to allow you to completely automate your build processes. You will also have more apps at your disposal than Cloud, and their licensing will be permanent.

- **Bitbucket Data Center:** The Enterprise offering from Bitbucket resembles a single instance of Bitbucket Server for its users, even though it is hosted on a significant number of servers within a cluster of your own environment. This leads to significant advantages like:

- **Performance at Scale:** Because a cluster of multiple machines running the Bitbucket Server should be able to handle more load than a single machine possibly could.

- **High Availability:** Because if one cluster node happens to go down, then the rest of the cluster nodes should be able to still continue servicing requests for users so that there is little to no loss of availability.

- **Smart Mirroring:** Smart Mirror should be able to improve Git clone speeds, particularly for distributed teams that continue to work with huge repositories.

Pull Requests with special features like in-line commenting to enhance the spirit as well as the practicality of collaboration between the different members of a software development team.

Appraisal

We have studied a lot of topics pertaining to Git in this book. Now, let us briefly go over the contents of this text so that we can revise and restate the facts and the information about Git that we studied.

Chapter 1 began with us talking about the basics of Version Control, what it is "A version control is a kind of system which allows you to keep track of the changes that have been made to a code over a duration of time. Making use of version control comes with its advantages. A version control software will keep track of all the changes that have been made to a code in a special, specific database. This means that you can, at any given point in time, revert back to the older versions of the code you are working on." Given its role in the world of technology in its present shape and form, VCS also ensures a significant increase in successful deployments as well as a reduction in development time. This makes them especially useful for DevOps teams, who are responsible for combining software development with IT operations. Some types are "SCM (Source Code Management) tools" and "RCS (Revision Control System)."

DOI: 10.1201/9781003229100-9

The next section focused on the eponymous concern of this textbook Git. We learnt that "Git is a Version Control software meant for tracking changes in a given set of files, for ensuring coordinated work among programmers who are collaboratively developing a source code for software development," and that "Its proposed goals are speed, support for distributed, non-linear workflows, as well as data integrity." A crucial reason as to why the software is so quick is that it does require regular access to the Internet to be able to function. If you are working on your system, you already have a copy of your master branch, so you will make the required set of changes on it without having to be online. Of course, you will have to push and pull changes at some point of time, ideally consistently and regularly, and that will require access to the Internet since we will have to interact with other systems and networks. Now, let's recall what pushing and pulling were. The push command implies the pushing of the contents of a local repository to a remote repository. The push command is used after a local repository is modified, and so these changes need to be shared with the other team members for them to work on an up-to-date code. Pull, on the other hand, moves in the opposite direction (obviously). A Pull command is to be utilized in order to fetch as well as merge changes from remote repository to the local repository.

The pull command has been recognized as a fusion of two different commands, git fetch as well as the git merge command, one followed by the other. The Git fetch command is able to download the required code from the remote repository, while the Git Merge command helps in combining the multiple changesets of both the branches into a single, seamless code line. We also came to about the different objects within the object database, the three main stages that our file will belong to within this software "Modified, Staged, and Committed," the "three central sections of any Git project – the working tree, the staging area, and the Git directory," etc. Quick definitions. What is a working tree? A working tree, also known as a working directory, consists of all the files that you are working on at the present moment. What, then, is a staging area? A staging area, or index, is a location of commit-preparation. The index conducts comparisons of the files present in the working tree with the files of the repository. And working directory? A working directory, .gitfolder in Git, constitutes all the information that is important for your project's version control, all the information regarding your commits, remote repositories, etc. The working directory, for example, will have a log storing your commit history so that you can roll back to an older changeset if that is what your work demands.

Then, there were the sections on the advantages and the disadvantages of this software. We were told about Git's better speed, its ease in "leverage third parties as well as encouraging them to fork their own open-source code," how the "shorter development cycle allows Git to synchronize multiple activities with separate releases," as well as how its "Graphical User Interface (GUI) is not effective and difficult to maneuver through," how it cannot "keep track of empty folders and suffers due to a lack of Windows support," "cannot support binary files," along with comparing its features as a Version Control System (VCS) to other examples of Version Control softwares like Perforce and Subversion. Brief details on the last two. Perforce or Perforce Software, Inc. is a software developer known for its version control system, developer collaboration, web application services, among others. Subversion, i.e. Apache Subversion too is a software versioning as well as revision control system distributed open source under the Apache License.

The section on the history of Git gave us an extensive background on what went into the creation of the VCS, as well as the circumstances that triggered creator Torvalds to go on a working vacation and come back with the code of this new VCS modeled after Larry McVoy's BitKeeper, some of the goals that the developers had in mind, like speed, the role of distribution, an ability to handle massive projects like the Linux kernel with a fair degree of efficiency and agility, a simple design, a healthy space for non-linear development, etc.

In Chapter 2, we transitioned toward understanding the practical uses of Git, particularly how it is to be installed, set up, as well as the tips and troubleshooting techniques bound to come in handy while making use of the VCS in our workspaces. We understood how we could install Git on Linux through a binary installer, how the "official Git website is also the go-to place for installing Git on Windows," how we need to go about setting up our usernames and passwords, the commands to be used in order to create a new repo, for cloning, use of git push, autocorrection, counting of commits, data-backup, use of tags, and many, many more. Remember Tags?

From Chapter 3 onward, we started going into details regarding each and every aspect of Git. Here, we learnt that

"Repositories in Git refer to a collection of files that contain the different versions of the same project" and that "These files are imported from the repository to the node, i.e. the local system of the developers for further changes and developments to the contents of the file." We learnt that a "working tree refers to a set of files that have originated from a particular version of a repository" as well as about the different stages a file tends to go through in the working tree of a Git repository. We learnt about how we could record changes in our repositories, as well as some remote management tips like showing remotes, adding remote repositories, pushing to the remotes, inspecting remotes, removing as well as renaming them, etc.

The next section focused on Git Aliases. We learned about how aliases were basically the short forms for a plethora of commands that we were bound to use while working on Git, how they saved time and improved efficiency, preserving our keystroke power, how the new commands created were supplements and could not replace the original form of commands, as it was. We also learned aspects of the topic like how we could create aliases for a range of commands, how aliases should ideally be used for the most used commands, inter alia. Next section involved the practice of Tagging and "how it involves the use of the git tag command." The central concern at hand was defined succinctly "Tagging is utilized to capture a particular point in history, and made use of for a marked version release. A tag, then, is a branch that is immune to any kind of change. Tags, unlike branches, will not have a history of commits after being created" and we learnt about the commands to go for in order to be able to list our tags, along with how to check out, share, delete them, etc. Further, we also learned about the kind of tags that are at our disposal in Git, the lightweight tags as well as the annotated tags.

In Chapter 4, our focus shifted to Branches. We learned that "A branch is supposed to be a copy of a code line, which is to be managed by the Version Control System (VCS)" as well as how "Branches allow for parallel work, along with a well-demarcated separation of work-in-progress code with the stable as well as tried-and-tested code." We were told about the set of instructions and commands we were supposed to employ while working with/on branches, whether it is the creation of branches or remote branches, deleting them, conducting merges, etc. While learning about concepts like Git Branching, we understood that there was nothing exceptional about the main branch as compared to the other branches, it was simply an initializing mechanism, a trunk that is supposed to give birth to several other branches. We also went in-depth attempting to amplify our definition as well as understanding of version control. We learned that every new branch was simply the announcement of a new pointer, and that Git as a software was keeping track of these successive pointers, one after the other, thus managing to keep a record of all the versions of the file that were now being made. We learned how branches often were called feature branches since a developer would work on a node (local system) in order to make changes to the code of a particular feature of a product, like a bug fix, a new development to be launched in the market, etc. It is also of incredible importance that the changes we make in our branch get pushed toward the central repository at regular intervals so that the trunk code is regularly updated, and there is less possibility of merge conflicts later on. With a proper example, we were able to demonstrate how branches facilitate independent work in tandem with a spirit of collaboration vis-à-vis the field of software development.

Chapter 5 was all about servers. We learned about the steps as well as the processes and complications involved in getting Git on server, putting the bare repository on a server, as well as how Git makes effective use of SSH access. Basically, an SSH key is supposed to be a kind of an access credential for the secure shell network protocol. The secure shell protocol is an authenticated as well as encrypted secure network protocol meant to be used on an unsecure open network in order to make remote communication possible. Various functions and facilities that SSH can help with regard to are network management, remote file transfer, as well as remote operating system access. The chapter then informed us about the different kinds of workflows that were possible on Git, like the Distributed Workflow, the Centralized Workflow, Integrator-Manager Workflow, and the Dictator and Lieutenants Workflow. The salient features of all of these systems were provided.

Chapters 6–8 focused on the important software companies/hosts spawned by the rip-roaring success of Git, namely GitHub, GitLab, as well as Bitbucket. For all of the three, we learned what their chief features were, the history associated with their softwares as well as the companies controlling and maintaining the codes, how we can go about operating the tools they offer, with a number of step-by-step processes for different functions, as well as the different kinds of accounts they offer to their users.

The invention of Git was nothing less than a miracle, a remarkable innovation that resolved a variety of issues that the coders had been struggling with for a really long period of time. While this books acts as a good primer to learn about the central concepts involved in this juggernaut, you are also recommended to continue on your journey as a learner as well as a developer, and master this beast well and proper. Good Luck!

Index